S0-BIJ-188

Great American Writers

TWENTIETH CENTURY

EDITOR

R. BAIRD SHUMAN

University of Illinois

John Steinbeck • Wallace Stevens
William Styron • Amy Tan • Studs Terkel
Anne Tyler • Alice Walker

MARSHALL CAVENDISH

NEW YORK • TORONTO • LONDON • SYDNEY

Marshall Cavendish
99 White Plains Road
Tarrytown, New York 10591-9001

Website: www.marshallcavendish.com

© 2002 Marshall Cavendish Corporation

All rights reserved. No part of this book may be reproduced or utilized in any form or by any means electronic or mechanical, including photocopying, recording, or by an information storage and re-trieval system, without prior written permission from the publisher and copyright holder.

Salem Press

    Editor: R. Baird Shuman
    Managing Editor: R. Kent Rasmussen

    Manuscript Editors: Heather Stratton
                        Lauren M. Mitchell
    Assistant Editor: Andrea Miller
    Research Supervisor: Jeffry Jensen
    Acquisitions Editor: Mark Rehn

Marshall Cavendish

    Project Editor: Marian Armstrong
    Editorial Director: Paul Bernabeo

Designer: Patrice Sheridan

Photo Research: Candlepants
                  Carousel Research
                  Linda Sykes Picture Research
                  Anne Burns Images

Indexing: AEIOU

Library of Congress Cataloging-in-Publication Data

Great American writers: twentieth century / R. Baird Shuman, editor.
    v. cm.
    Includes bibliographical references and indexes.
    Contents: v. 1. Agee-Bellow--v. 2. Benét-Cather--v. 3. Cormier-Dylan--v. 4. Eliot-Frost--v. 5. Gaines-Hinton--v. 6. Hughes-Lewis--v. 7. London-McNickle--v. 8. Miller-O'Connor--v. 9. O'Neill-Rich--v. 10. Salinger-Stein--v. 11. Steinbeck-Walker--v. 12. Welty-Zindel--v. 13. Index.
    ISBN 0-7614-7240-1 (set)—ISBN 0-7614-7251-7 (v. 11)
    1. American literature--20th century--Bio-bibliography--Dictionaries. 2. Authors, American--20th century--Biography--Dictionaries. 3. American literature--20th century--Dictionaries. I. Shuman, R. Baird (Robert Baird), 1929-

PS221.G74 2002
810.9'005'03
[B]   2001028461

Printed in Malaysia; bound in the United States

07 06 05 04 03 02   6 5 4 3 2 1

Volume 11 Illustration Credits
(a = above, b = below, l = left, r = right)

AP/Wide World Photos: 1508
Archive Photos: 1544, 1571
Art Resource, NY: 1533
Jonathan Blair/Corbis: 1452
Bridgeman Art Library/Private Collection/Christie's Images: 1526
Bridgeman Art Library/Private Collection/Michael Graham Stewart: 1574
Courtesy Sue and Clayton Bruntz: 1465
John Bunker/SuperStock: 1559
Noah Burger/AP/Wide World Photos: 1569
Frank Capri/Archive Photos: cover portrait of Alice Walker, 1561
Corbis: 1487, 1525, 1539
Corbis/Bettmann: 1447, 1449, 1455, 1461, 1491, 1492, 1495, 1522, 1528, 1530, 1564, 1565
William Coupon/Gamma Liaison: 1493 (r)
Terry Cryer/Corbis: 1531
David David Gallery, Philadelphia/SuperStock: 1578
Steven Deutch/Chicago Historical Society: 1529
The Dorothea Lange Collection, The Oakland Museum of California, The City of Oakland. Gift of Paul S. Taylor. Neg. # 33001: 1448
Duke University Archives: 1543
Duke University Rare Book, Manuscript & Special Collections Library: 1490
Ron Edmonds/AP/Wide World Photos: 1521
Essen Museum, Germany/SuperStock: 1577
Michael Ferguson/Globe Photos, Inc.: cover portrait of Amy Tan, 1505
Fine Art Photographic Library, London/Art Resource, NY: 1472
Giraudon/Art Resource, NY: 1474, 1484
Bernard Gotfryd/Archive Photos: 1494
Elizabeth Barakah Hodges/SuperStock: 1581
Hulton-Deutsch Collection/Corbis: 1450
The Huntington Library, San Marino, California: 1469, 1470
The Huntington Library, San Marino, California/Bachrach: 1468
The Huntington Library, San Marino, California/Pach Brothers: cover portrait of Wallace Stevens, 1467
Image Select/Art Resource, NY: 1538, 1554
James M. Kelly/Globe Photos, Inc.: 1493 (l)
Kelly-Mooney Photography/Corbis: cover portrait of Studs Terkel, 1519
Private Collection, Dale Kennington/SuperStock: 1556
Kordray Foltz Collection/The Georgia Historical Society: 1562
Library of Congress, Neg. # USF 34-16113: 1453
Library of Congress, Neg. # USF 342701-16453: 1463
Craig Lovell/Corbis: 1458
Private Collection, Donald C. Martin/SuperStock: 1553
Court Mast/AP/Wide World Photos: 1567
Dominique Nabokov/Gamma Liaison: cover portrait of William Styron, 1489
National Portrait Gallery, Smithsonian Institution/Art Resource, NY: 1502
The New Press: 1522, 1523
New York Times/Archive Photos: 1573
North Carolina Division of Archives and History: 1542, 1549
Naoki Okamoto/SuperStock: 1512
Diana Ong/SuperStock: 1524, 1548, 1550
Penguin Books: 1451, 1454
"Berkeley Cover," copyright © 1988 by ATM, Inc., from *Breathing Lessons* by Anne Tyler. Used by permission of Berkeley Publishing Group, a division of Penguin Putnam Inc.: 1546
"Berkeley Cover," copyright © 1985 by Anne Tyler Modarressi, et. Al., from *The Accidental Tourist* by Anne Tyler. Used by permission of Berkeley Publishing Group, a division of Penguin Putnam Inc.: 1551
From *The Joy Luck Club* by Amy Tan, copyright © 1989 by Amy Tan. Used by permission of G. P. Putnam's Sons, a division of Penguin Putnam Inc.: 1509
Petit Palais, Geneva/SuperStock: 1568
Photofest: 1457, 1459, 1506, 1513, 1520
Popperfoto/Archive Photos: cover portrait of John Steinbeck, 1445
Zifen Qian/SuperStock: 1511
Reprinted by permission of Vintage Books and Ballantine Books, Divisions of Random House, Inc.: 1475, 1496, 1500, 1514, 1575
Reuters NewMedia Inc.: 1477
Charles E. Rotkin/Corbis: 1507
San Jose State University Center for Steinbeck Studies: 1446
Scala/Art Resource, NY: 1483, 1515, 1547, 1580
Susanne Schuenke/SuperStock: 1485
Sickles Photo Reporting/SuperStock: 1479
Smithsonian American Art Museum, Washington, D.C./Art Resource, NY: 1473, 1497, 1499, 1537
Snark/Art Resource, NY: 1535
Spelman College Archives: 1563
SuperStock: 1480
Tate Gallery, London/SuperStock: 1486
Diana Walker/Gamma Liaison: 1545
Diana Walker/TimePix: cover portrait of Anne Tyler, 1541
Warner Brothers: 1566
Warner Brothers/Archive Photos: 1570
Anna Belle Lee Washington/SuperStock: 1503
Michael C. York/AP/Wide World Photos: 1510

Contents

John Steinbeck   *1445*

Wallace Stevens   *1469*

William Styron   *1489*

Amy Tan   *1505*

Studs Terkel   *1521*

Anne Tyler   *1543*

Alice Walker   *1561*

Volume Index   1583

John Steinbeck

BORN: February 27, 1902, Salinas, California
DIED: December 20, 1968, New York, New York
IDENTIFICATION: Mid-twentieth century California novelist best known for his socially conscious books, several of which were made into classic films.

Steinbeck wrote his most popular and most critically praised books during the Great Depression years of the 1930s. *The Grapes of Wrath* (1939), his most important book by all measures, stirred the conscience of America with its painfully accurate depiction of a poor family fleeing Oklahoma's Dust Bowl to find work in California. Although Steinbeck's later work did not enjoy the same critical and popular success as his early work, he became only the sixth American writer awarded a Nobel Prize in Literature in 1962. By the end of the century, more than three decades after his death, his books were still widely read, with many being regularly taught in school and college classrooms.

The Writer's Life

On February 27, 1902, John Ernst Steinbeck III was born in a modest frame house in the central California town of Salinas. He was the third of four children and only son of John Ernst and Olive Hamilton Steinbeck.

Steinbeck's father was not wealthy and lacked business skills but was, however, thrifty and honest. When Steinbeck was eight, his father's feed store failed, and neighbors rallied to the family's support. Later his father became treasurer of Monterey County. This position gave the family a sense of security and sustained his father through the rest of his life.

Although the elder Steinbeck had a stern outward demeanor, he did support his only son. He later enabled John to attend college and helped him financially through his difficult apprenticeship writing years. Steinbeck's father also sent two of his three daughters to college.

Childhood. While growing up in a loving and close-knit family, Steinbeck enjoyed a happy childhood in Salinas. A small but prosperous trading community, Salinas stands only fifteen miles inland from the picturesque Monterey Peninsula. With its beautiful golden hills and temperate climate, the region served as an inspiration to Steinbeck after he became a writer. As a boy, he especially enjoyed spending time at the nearby ranch of his grandparents, where his mother had grown up.

The Future Writer. Steinbeck's interest in writing grew out of his early reading. From his schoolteacher mother he learned Bible stories at an early age. She also introduced him to tales from such works as the Arabian Nights and the epic poetry of John Milton. On his ninth birthday, she gave him a copy of Sir Thomas Malory's *Le Morte d'Arthur*, a fifteenth-century collection of stories about England's legendary King Arthur and his Round Table. By Steinbeck's early teens, he had decided to become a writer. It was a decision from which he never wavered.

College Years. After graduating from Salinas High School in 1919, Steinbeck entered Stanford University in nearby Palo Alto. He enrolled as an English major, although his father wanted him to study something he considered practical, such as engineering or business. Attending classes sporadically over the next six years, Steinbeck spent much of his time on academic probation.

In 1925 Steinbeck left Stanford so he could concentrate on writing. He did not graduate, but his college years exposed him to challenging literature. His college years gave him time to read, think, and

The streets of Salinas, California, Steinbeck's hometown. Taken in the early 1900s, this photograph captures how the town looked when Steinbeck was a child.

exchange ideas with the many bright people around him. He wrote constantly while at Stanford but published only five satirical poems and stories in campus publications.

The Fledgling Writer. After quitting Stanford, Steinbeck traveled east for the first time, sailing through the Panama Canal and up the East Coast to New York City. Still hoping to establish himself as a writer, he took a construction job, helping to build the famous Madison Square Garden. He then worked briefly for *The American*, a Hearst newspaper.

After returning to California in 1926, Steinbeck was troubled by a publisher's rejection of his first book of short stories. He retreated to Lake Tahoe in the Sierra Nevada range. There he worked as a lodge caretaker and wrote in solitude. In 1929 he finally published his first book, *Cup of Gold*, a novel he had begun at Stanford and rewritten six times. A story about the seventeenth-century English pirate Henry Morgan, this novel was heavily influenced by *Le Morte d'Arthur*. Like Malory's classic, his novel has a quest-for-the-Grail motif.

The Depression Years. A month after *Cup of Gold* was published, the New York stock market crashed, beginning the Great Depression that lasted through the 1930s. This was not a time when people had money to buy books, and *Cup of Gold* sold a paltry fifteen hundred copies. It, along with Steinbeck's next two novels, *The Pastures of Heaven* (1932) and *To a God Unknown* (1933), earned him a total of only nine hundred dollars. Nevertheless, Steinbeck sold the first two of three parts of *The Red Pony* to the *North American Review* in 1933. When one of his short stories was chosen as an O. Henry prize story in 1934, he received his first national recognition.

Tex Richard, a noted fight promoter, drives a gold-plated rivet into a girder at ceremonies marking the start of construction on the new Madison Square Garden in August 1925. Steinbeck, who helped build the structure, may have been among the swarms of excited construction workers and onlookers.

Marriage and Domestic Life. On January 14, 1930, Steinbeck married the first of his three wives, Carol Henning. They settled in a Pacific Grove house on the Monterey Peninsula owned by his father, who also provided a twenty-five-dollar-a-month allowance. Steinbeck soon met Ed Ricketts, who became his closest friend (and the model for characters in three future Steinbeck books). Ricketts owned a biological supply company on Monterey's Cannery Row. Later, the two friends would explore the Sea of Cortez off Baja California and together write a nonfiction book about their trip.

The Turning Point. Steinbeck finally published his first successful book, *Tortilla Flat*, in 1935. This novel is an Arthurian-inspired legend about Mexican American drifters living near Monterey. He had trouble getting the new book published, but it won a prize as the best book of the year by a Californian. In addition, Metro-Goldwyn-Mayer (MGM) bought its movie rights for several thousand dollars—the most money Steinbeck had earned to that point. His fortunes were finally rising.

Steinbeck's name was emerging when few people had money to buy books. This photograph of a man standing on a breadline during the Great Depression places the mindset of the times in perspective.

Growing Interest in Social Issues.

Around this same time, Steinbeck was hired by the *San Francisco News* to write articles about California's migrant worker camps. In 1936 he published *In Dubious Battle*, a novel about a farmworker strike. Using material he collected for his newspaper articles, he published both *The Long Valley*, a short story collection, and *Their Blood Is Strong*, containing articles about migrant labor camps, in 1938.

Steinbeck's field research also helped inspire him to write his most celebrated novel, *The Grapes of Wrath* (1939), which won a Pulitzer Prize and an American Booksellers' Award and was made into a major film. Selling more than a half million copies in its original edition, the book brought Steinbeck sudden wealth.

Writing Successes and Family Failures.

The resounding success of *The Grapes of Wrath* suddenly made Steinbeck a public figure and placed new strains on his family life. In 1935 he had built a new house in Los Gatos, California, so he and his wife could live closer to her hometown of San Jose. However, their marriage did not survive the changes that came with Steinbeck's success. New demands on his time, including work on a film in Mexico, kept him away from home so much that Carol divorced him in 1942.

The following year, Steinbeck married Gwyn Conger, with whom he moved to New York City. They had two sons, Thom (born in 1944) and John IV (1946). This marriage did not last either. In 1948, when Steinbeck returned from a trip to California, Gwyn asked him for a divorce. She and the boys returned to California, leaving Steinbeck, who had recently undergone painful back surgery, bereft. During that same difficult year, his good friend Ed Ricketts was killed in a car accident.

Rebuilding His Life.

Although Steinbeck's personal life was a shambles, he continued writing regularly, turning out such books as *Bombs Away!* (1942), *The Moon Is Down* (1942), *Cannery Row* (1945), *The Pearl* (1947), *The Wayward Bus* (1947), and *A Russian Journal* (1948). Valuing the anonymity that New York provided him, he never again lived in California. On December 29, 1950, he married Elaine Anderson Scott, a woman fully sensitive to his artistic needs. She stayed with him until he died.

Last Years.

During Steinbeck's last eighteen years, he lived in both New York City and Sag Harbor on nearby Long Island. The novels he wrote through these years were generally not well received, but he kept working. Meanwhile, films made from his books generally fared better than the books themselves. Particularly successful was the film adaptation of his novel *East of Eden* (1952), which introduced actor James Dean in 1955.

Steinbeck's most popular book during his last years was his beguiling account of a cross-country trip he made with his dog, *Travels with Charley: In Search of America* (1962). That same

Steinbeck and his third wife, Elaine, posing for a picture on the sunporch of their home in Sag Harbor, New York, in 1962.

FILMS BASED ON STEINBECK'S STORIES

1939 Of Mice and Men

1940 The Grapes of Wrath

1942 Tortilla Flat

1943 The Moon Is Down

1944 Lifeboat

1945 A Medal for Benny

1947 The Pearl

1949 The Red Pony

1955 East of Eden

1957 The Wayward Bus

1959 Burning Bright (TV)

1961 Flight

1971 The Harness (TV)

1973 The Red Pony (TV)

1981 East of Eden (TV miniseries)

1981 Of Mice and Men (TV)

1982 Cannery Row

1983 The Winter of Our Discontent (TV)

1991 The Grapes of Wrath (TV)

1992 Of Mice and Men

year, he was awarded the Nobel Prize in Literature. The award surprised many people—including Steinbeck himself—because his literary reputation had by then greatly declined.

In 1967 Steinbeck had surgery on his back from which he never fully recovered. On December 20, 1968, he died in New York City, giving in to health problems that had especially plagued him through his last year and a half. His body was returned to California for burial in Salinas, where his birthplace was later made into a museum.

The Writer's Work

John Steinbeck wrote long and short fiction, nonfiction, plays, and screenplays. He is, however, known primarily for his long fiction, particularly his novels of the 1930s. The most conspicuous qualities of these novels are their supple narrative style, the rich variety of subject matter, and Steinbeck's steadfast sympathy for common people.

Issues in Steinbeck's Fiction. Steinbeck once declared that a writer should record "his time as nearly as he can understand it." He added that a writer should also "serve as the watchdog of society . . . to satirize its silliness, to attack its injustices, to stigmatize its faults." Steinbeck's best books do all those things—and in ways that have compelled millions of people to read them. Focusing mostly on social problems brought by the Great Depression, those books have made Steinbeck the leading American literary spokesperson for the social ills of the 1930s.

Steinbeck happened to come to maturity as a writer at a time when the Depression was forcing a reevaluation of the American dream. With banks, businesses, and farms failing across the nation, millions of people were put out of work, and it appeared that the entire country might sink into poverty. In the midst of that desperate moment in the nation's history, Steinbeck took on issues that were at once controversial and rich with dramatic potential: poverty, unfair labor practices, homelessness, and failed dreams. His books were controversial when they were published, but people read them avidly because they accurately portrayed painful truths. Indeed, the books have a unique and permanent value as social commentary on American life.

People in Steinbeck's Fiction. Steinbeck's finest fictional characters are ordinary people in extraordinary situa-

tions. Typically poor or working class, they struggle to survive on the fringes of society. Characters in his books set in the 1930s respond to terrible economic conditions realistically, but not without a strong element of romantic, intuitive escape. More than mere victims of social or economic failure, they celebrate a life-force beyond society and economics. Supported by a consistent narrative tone, Steinbeck's best books maintain powerful tensions between the worlds of harsh reality and animal-like freedom.

Among Steinbeck's most memorable characters are Lennie and George, the itinerant ranch workers in *Of Mice and Men* (1937) who dream of having their own farm; the carefree "paisanos" in *Tortilla Flat*; the colorful residents of Monterey's Cannery Row; the self-sacrificing strike leaders of *In Dubious Battle*; and the impoverished Joads in *The Grapes of*

Steinbeck, seen here around 1930, set his sights on becoming a writer at an early age. Although his father wished a more practical career for his son, Steinbeck was married to the idea of becoming a writer.

HIGHLIGHTS IN STEINBECK'S LIFE

1902   John Steinbeck III is born on February 27 in Salinas, California.

1919   Graduates from Salinas High School; enters Stanford University.

1920–1925 Works part time and summers doing maintenance work for a Salinas sugar company.

1925   Works in New York City.

1926–1928 Spends summers living at Lake Tahoe.

1929   Publishes first novel, *Cup of Gold.*

1930   Marries Carol Henning and settles on Monterey Peninsula; continues writing and publishing.

1934   Begins field research among farmworkers.

1937   Makes first trip to Europe.

1939   Publishes his most successful book, *The Grapes of Wrath.*

1940   Visits Baja California with Ed Ricketts; receives National Book Award and Pulitzer Prize for *The Grapes of Wrath.*

1941   Moves to New York City with Gwyn Conger.

1942   Is divorced by Carol.

1943   Marries Gwyn; serves as war correspondent in Europe and North Africa.

1944   First son, Thom, is born.

1946   Second son, John IV, is born.

1947   Steinbeck visits Russia.

1948   Steinbeck is divorced by Gwyn; Ricketts dies.

1950   Steinbeck marries Elaine Anderson Scott.

1959   Researches background for a modern version of *Le Morte d'Arthur* in Great Britain.

1960   Drives around the United States with his dog, Charley.

1962   Receives Nobel Prize in Literature.

1963   Travels in Europe.

1964   Awarded the U.S. Medal of Freedom by President Lyndon B. Johnson.

1968   Dies in New York on December 20; is buried in Salinas.

1974   His Salinas birthplace house becomes a public museum.

1979   U.S. Postal Service issues a Steinbeck commemorative stamp.

JOHN STEINBECK
The Grapes of Wrath

Wrath. All these people are cut off from society's mainstream in one way or another but still retain idealistic visions that give them strength. Steinbeck brings them to life by portraying them with unerring mixtures of realism and romance.

Steinbeck discovered the dignity of labor and common people through his own experiences. During his youth, he worked, intermittently, as a ranch hand, menial laborer, and construction worker. Through actual jobs and his journalistic research, he got to know, firsthand, members of California's Mexican American community, migrant farmworkers, and other common laborers. His respect for such people is apparent throughout his fiction.

Steinbeck achieved his greatest literary success in 1939 with *The Grapes of Wrath,* his heart-rending story about an Oklahoma farming family's futile quest to find the promised land in California. The most powerful and eloquent expression of his concern for common people, that book was also his last major work on that theme. It is difficult for any author to follow a triumph as great as *The Grapes of Wrath.* Almost everything Steinbeck wrote after it was judged by its standards and came up short.

The Theme of Disillusionment. The theme of gaining what one has always wanted only to be disillusioned on its attainment is also com-

SOME INSPIRATIONS BEHIND STEINBECK'S WORK

All authors are motivated by the people, places, and experiences that help shape them. In John Steinbeck's case, it is apparent that his schoolteacher mother, who first encouraged him to read great literature, served as an important early influence and inspiration. Beginning with the Bible and the classics, she made reading an integral part of his early life. The influence of his early reading was apparent until the end of his life, when he was working on his own version of Sir Thomas Malory's *Le Morte d'Arthur.*

Steinbeck grew up in the Salinas Valley and was also familiar with the nearby Monterey Peninsula and the woods of Big Sur to its south. He frequently returned to those places in his writing. He was especially familiar with the central California ranch on which his mother grew up. The stories of *The Red Pony* are set near it, as are *Of Mice and Men* and *East of Eden.*

When Steinbeck was commissioned to explore migrant worker camps for the *San Francisco News,* he became emotionally and intellectually involved with the oppressed people he met while doing his field research. He had grown up around simple, commonplace people, and was at his literary best in their company.

Ed Ricketts, who owned a biological laboratory on Monterey's Cannery Row, became Steinbeck's closest friend and remained so from their first meeting in 1930 until his death in 1948. Ricketts was the main inspiration for the protagonist, Doc, in *Cannery Row* and appears in other Steinbeck novels and stories.

The Big Sur coastline in the fog. Ed Ricketts, Steinbeck's dearest friend, saw the force of the sea as the underlying energy of life. "Wave motion gave life its original direction," he said. "It's built into every one of our cells." Several of Steinbeck's characters were modeled after Ricketts, and the scenic beauty of Big Sur was always a faithful source of inspiration.

mon throughout Steinbeck's work. In *The Grapes of Wrath*, for example, the Joads achieve their dream of reaching California, but once they arrive, that dream crumbles. In *The Red Pony*, Jody gets the pony for which he has long hankered, only to see it die. In *Tortilla Flat*, Danny becomes a property owner, but ownership brings him only grief and friction with his friends.

Similar disillusionment themes pervade American literature. Stories from Herman Melville's *Moby Dick* (1851) to Ernest Hemingway's *The Old Man and the Sea* (1952) explore this theme, always reaching the same conclusion: The quest is what matters; attainment leads inevitably to disappointment.

Steinbeck and Film. Steinbeck's direct involvement with the film industry was extensive, and his work has continued to be adapted to the screen since his death. A dozen of his stories have been made into feature-length films and television movies. Two feature films used screenplays he wrote himself—*The Pearl* (1947) and *The Red Pony* (1949). (Steinbeck also wrote the screenplay for his short story "Lifeboat" but insisted that his name be removed from the film's credits.)

When writing *Of Mice and Men*, Steinbeck developed the technique of writing a novel that could easily be adapted to stage or screen. Making full use of the dramatic and documentary techniques he had mastered as early as the mid-1930s, he later wrote the original screenplays for *The Forgotten Village* (1941) and *Viva Zapata!* (1952).

Steinbeck's Literary Legacy. Although Steinbeck died in 1968, it may be too early to assign him his place in American literary history. His work has attracted considerable atten-

Steinbeck's respect for common, hardworking people, such as this man crouching at the edge of a pea field in 1937, is evident throughout the body of his work. Steinbeck's scrutiny of poverty and unfair labor practices is his prevailing literary theme.

tion. It has always appealed to general readers, as well as some academic critics, and has become standard curriculum fare at the junior high, high school, and college levels. However, many academic critics dismiss his work as no longer important.

Regardless of how Steinbeck is eventually judged, one categorical claim can be made: He will long be remembered for his humanity and for his nonjudgmental and sympathetic depiction of people forced to live on the fringes of American society. Steinbeck was—and will likely remain—the preeminent American novelist of the Great Depression. No other writer has better exposed the dark underside of the American dream. At the same time, few novelists have matched his ability to celebrate the human hopes symbolized in that dream. While Steinbeck's best fictional works depict a paradise

LONG FICTION

1929 Cup of Gold
1932 The Pastures of Heaven
1933 To a God Unknown
1935 Tortilla Flat
1936 In Dubious Battle
1937 The Red Pony
1937 Of Mice and Men
1939 The Grapes of Wrath
1942 The Moon Is Down
1945 Cannery Row
1945 The Pearl (serialized in 1945; book in 1947)
1947 The Wayward Bus
1950 Burning Bright
1952 East of Eden
1954 Sweet Thursday
1957 The Short Reign of Pippen IV
1961 The Winter of Our Discontent
1976 Acts of King Arthur and His Noble Knights, edited by Horton Chase

SHORT FICTION

1936 Saint Katy the Virgin
1938 The Long Valley

PLAYS

1937 Of Mice and Men
1942 The Moon Is Down
1951 Burning Bright

SCREENPLAYS

1941 The Forgotten Village
1944 Lifeboat (uncredited)
1945 A Medal for Benny
1945 The Pearl
1949 The Red Pony
1952 Viva Zapata!

NONFICTION

1938 Their Blood Is Strong
1941 The Forgotten Village
1941 Sea of Cortez (with Edward F. Ricketts)
1942 Bombs Away

1948 A Russian Journal (with Robert Capa)
1958 Once There Was a War
1962 Travels with Charley: In Search of America
1965 Letters to Alicia
1966 America and Americans
1969 Journal of a Novel: The "East of Eden" Letters
1975 Steinbeck: A Life in Letters, ed. Elaine Steinbeck and Robert Wallsten

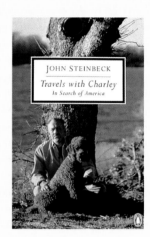

JOHN STEINBECK
Travels with Charley
In Search of America

lost, they also hold out the hope of a paradise to be regained. At their best, Steinbeck's books demonstrate a greatness of heart and mind rarely matched in modern American literature.

BIBLIOGRAPHY

Bloom, Harold, ed. *John Steinbeck*. New York: Chelsea House, 1987.

Fensch, Thomas, ed. *Conversations with John Steinbeck*. Jackson: University of Mississippi Press, 1988.

French, Warren. *John Steinbeck*. New York: Twayne Publishers, 1961; revised and enlarged, 1975.

———. *John Steinbeck's Fiction Revisited*. New York: Twayne Publishers, 1994.

———. *John Steinbeck's Nonfiction Revisited*. New York: Twayne Publishers, 1996.

Hayashi, Tetsumaro, ed. *John Steinbeck: The Years of Greatness, 1936–1939*. Tuscaloosa: University of Alabama Press, 1993.

Lisca, Peter. *The Wide World of John Steinbeck*. New Brunswick, N.J.: Rutgers University Press, 1958.

Marks, Lester Jay. *Thematic Design in the Novels of John Steinbeck*. The Hague: Mouton, 1969.

McElrath, Joseph R., J. S. Crisler, and Susan Shillinglaw, eds. *John Steinbeck: The Contemporary Reviews*. New York: Cambridge University Press, 1996.

Millchap, Joseph R. *Steinbeck and Film*. New York: Frederick Ungar, 1983.

Parini, Jay. *John Steinbeck: A Biography*. New York: Henry Holt, 1995.

Railsback, Brian, ed. *The John Steinbeck Encyclopedia*. Westport, Conn.: Greenwood Press, 1996.

Filming The Grapes of Wrath

The only American novel of the 1930s whose popularity can be compared to that of *The Grapes of Wrath* was Margaret Mitchell's *Gone with the Wind* (1936). Like *Gone with the Wind*, *The Grapes of Wrath* was bought by a film studio and rushed into production. David O. Selznick bought the rights to Mitchell's novel, and Darryl F. Zanuck bought the rights to Steinbeck's. Zanuck hired Nunnally Johnson to write the screenplay, Alfred Newman to provide the musical score, and John Ford to direct the film. *The Grapes of Wrath* was shot on Twentieth Century Fox's backlot in Southern California in late 1939 and released on January 24, 1940.

The film's cast was stellar. Henry Fonda, who later became one of Steinbeck's closest friends, had the lead role as Tom Joad. Jane Darwell played Ma Joad and won an Academy Award as best supporting actress for her performance. John Carradine played Jim Casy. The film was not flawless, but its entire cast turned in superb performances. Although the film's sound quality was substandard and hasty editing, necessitated by the rush to get the film into theaters resulted in some choppiness, the sheer strength of Steinbeck's epic story overcame these technical weaknesses.

Fact into Fiction. In his early career, Steinbeck was a documentarian, as *Their Blood Is Strong* (1938),

Actor Henry Fonda, seen here on the set of the film adaptation of *The Grapes of Wrath*, gave one of the most memorable performances of his career when he played the role of Tom Joad.

which predates *The Grapes of Wrath*, reveals. The earlier book, a collection of nonfiction pieces about migrant workers written for the *San Francisco News*, is clearly documentary in nature. Steinbeck decided to turn his nonfiction pieces into a realistic novel because in that genre he would be able to shape the socioeconomic emphasis of the book better than he would if he were writing a strict documentary. He pointed out at the time that most documentaries are about large groups of people and contended that, in a novel, readers can identify more closely with individuals than they can with the large groups in documentaries.

Before Zanuck bought the film rights for the novel, he sent private detectives into the field to investigate the conditions that Steinbeck depicted among farmworkers. Zanuck's detectives reported not only that the terrible conditions described in *The Grapes of Wrath* were true but that the real conditions were frequently even worse than Steinbeck had portrayed them.

Novel Versus Film Script. Whereas Lewis Milestone's *Of Mice and Men* remained extremely faithful to Steinbeck's novel, Ford and Johnson took liberties with his work and for various reasons were forced to omit crucial details from their screen version of *The Grapes of Wrath*. When Steinbeck wrote *Of Mice and Men*, he consciously wrote it in scenes that were adaptable, almost without revision, to dramatic presentation. Such was not the case in *The Grapes of Wrath*, a book that from the outset was highly controversial.

Steinbeck's novel evolved from an ironic and satirical story entitled *L'Affaire Lettuceberg* into an American epic. As director of the film version, Ford had an overall social philosophy fundamentally different from Steinbeck's.

Although Ford shared some populist sentiments born of the Great Depression, he was at heart a conservative. Rather than looking ahead to new worlds and new opportunities as Steinbeck did, Ford tended to dwell nostalgically on a lost past, hoping that it could be recaptured. He found in the institution of the nuclear family a thread that linked the past he hoped to recapture to the present. In Steinbeck's view, on the other hand, the crumbling nuclear family became universalized. This is shown in the novel's ending, when Rose of Sharon shares the milk from her breast with a starving man. This man, though not a member of her family, is part of the universal family of humankind that Steinbeck's social philosophy acknowledges and promotes.

The Revised Ending. Ford did not end the film version with Rose of Sharon's sharing the gift of life with a stranger in a barn. Such an ending would have evoked considerable controversy, but it also went against the grain of what Ford himself believed. Ford also followed a script that virtually ignored the novel's interchapters in which is found much of the philosophical content of *The Grapes of Wrath*. The film's cinematographer, Greg Toland, used clever photographic techniques as substitutes for Steinbeck's literary techniques, particularly in rela-

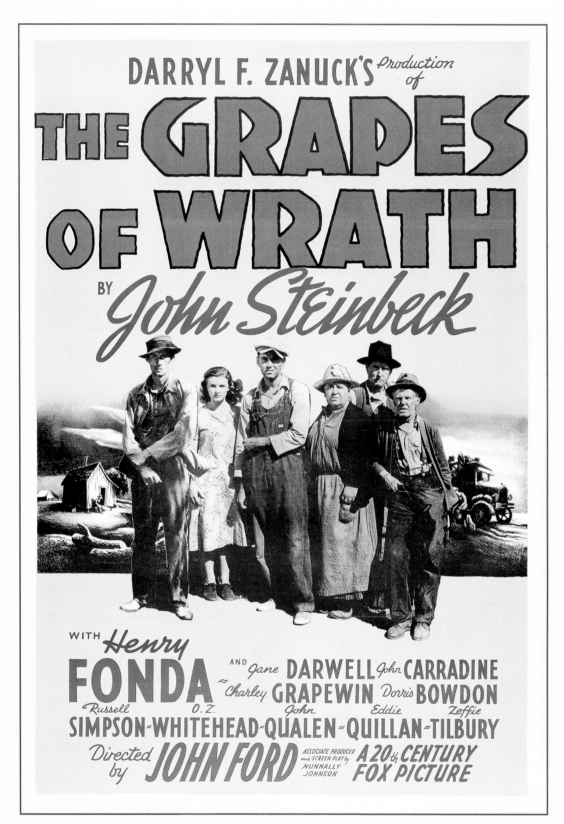

This splashy poster promoting the now-legendary film version of *The Grapes of Wrath* features the all-star cast, with actor Henry Fonda as Tom Joad front and center. The motion picture was released in 1940, just months after the publication of the novel.

These fertile hills in California represent the unattainable promised land.

tion to the material in the interchapters. One example is a brief scene showing a turtle—which symbolizes the migrants—crossing a road. After a woman driving a car swerves to miss the turtle, a truck driver alters his course to hit it.

Oklahoma's Chamber of Commerce attempted to block the production of the film, claiming that it was disparaging to Oklahoma. Tempers were so ignited by both the book and the film that Oklahoma representative Lyle H. Boren read a scathing denunciation of *The Grapes of Wrath* into the *Congressional Record*. Despite the ongoing controversy, however, both the novel and the film were resounding commercial successes and each made its mark artistically as well.

Commenting in 1958 on the films made from his novels, Steinbeck had no unkind words for John Ford or Nunnally Johnson. He reminded readers that books and films are two different kinds of media, each with its own conventions, demands, and techniques. There is no evidence that Steinbeck was displeased with Ford's version of *The Grapes of Wrath*.

SOURCES FOR FURTHER STUDY

Boren, Lyle H. "*The Grapes of Wrath*." *Congressional Record*, 85 (January 10, 1939), Part 13, pp. 139–140.

Fensch, Thomas. *Conversations with John Steinbeck*. Jackson: University of Mississippi Press, 1988.

Millichap, Joseph R. *Steinbeck and Film*. New York: Frederick Ungar, 1983.

Readers Guide to Major Works

TORTILLA FLAT

   Genre: Novel
   Subgenre: Picaresque tragicomedy
   Published: New York, 1935
   Time period: 1930s
   Setting: Monterey County, California

Themes and Issues. Although Steinbeck's first commercially successful novel is set among Mexican Americans (here called "paisanos") in an early-twentieth-century California fishing village, readers have long found Arthurian overtones in the book. Steinbeck himself claimed *Tortilla Flat* was patterned on Malory's *Le Morte d'Arthur.* He may have overstated his case to satisfy his critics, but his book does broadly resemble Malory's. In its preface Steinbeck wrote that "Danny's house was not unlike the Round Table, and Danny's friends were not unlike the knights of it." *Tortilla Flat* adopts Malory's style in its romantic chapter headings. For example, one chapter is headed: "How the poison of possessions wrought with Pilon and how evil temporarily triumphed in him."

The Plot. A resident of Monterey's poor Tortilla Flat district, Danny is generous and outgoing. He and his simple, nonjudgmental friends have no steady jobs but are loyal to each another. They live from day to day, ignoring clocks and the future, surviving however they can. Not acquisitive, Danny owns only what he needs to get along. His life suddenly changes,

Spencer Tracy (far left) played the role of Danny, the big-hearted homeowner, while actors John Garfield, Sheldon Leonard, and Akim Tamiroff (left to right) were members of the group of paisanos, or Mexican Americans, in the film version of Steinbeck's first successful novel, *Tortilla Flat.*

however, when his grandfather dies, leaving two modest houses to him.

When Danny moves into one of his new houses, he shares it with his friends. He appears to have the perfect arrangement—one house to live in and another to rent out. Soon, however, Danny's friends Pilon, Jesus Maria, and Pablo accidentally burn down one of the houses. Danny initially chastises his friends and calls them names. Later, however, he realizes that losing one house has lightened his ownership responsibilities, so he forgives his friends.

Having their own ethical codes, Danny's friends talk a man known as the "Pirate" into living with them. They hope that he will reveal where he hides the money that he has been hoarding so they can steal it. Eventually, however, the man entrusts his money to Danny's friends for safekeeping, explaining that he is saving to buy a candlestick for the church. Danny's friends decide they cannot steal from someone who shows them such trust.

Later Danny retreats into the forest. When he returns, he goes on a binge of drinking and vandalism, and sells his remaining house. His friends, feeling betrayed, regain the house through trickery while Danny goes to jail. After Danny is released, they throw a big party for him. Danny again gets drunk, rushes out to fight an unseen enemy, falls into a gulch, and dies.

Analysis. *Tortilla Flat* is notable as an ironic social critique of middle-class values. It also captures—with considerable sympathy and sentimentality—the early-twentieth-century milieu of California's remnant Mexican population. When Steinbeck compares his paisanos to the hardworking Anglo middle class, he does so ironically and with compassion and understanding. His novel is thus as much a critique of the middle class, viewed against the backdrop of Danny's society, as it is of Danny and his friends.

Following its publication in 1935, *Tortilla Flat* was widely misinterpreted. Appearing during the darkest days of the Great Depression, when millions of Americans were struggling to find work, it seemed to glorify ir-

responsibility. As a result, many critics shunned the book as offering no moral compass to readers. Steinbeck—who considered the book second-rate—offered to supply his agents with explanations in "interchapters" that would illuminate the moral, historical, and aesthetic meaning of the book's episodes, but *Tortilla Flat* was published without them. Despite early critical condemnation of the book, it proved to be Steinbeck's first commercial success and was made into a popular film, in which Spencer Tracy played Danny.

SOURCES FOR FURTHER STUDY

Benson, Jackson J., ed. *The Short Novels of John Steinbeck.* Durham, N.C.: Duke University Press, 1990.

DeMott, Robert. "Voltaire Didn't Like Anything: A 1939 Interview with John Steinbeck." In *Conversations with John Steinbeck,* edited by Thomas Fensch. Jackson: University of Mississippi Press, 1988.

Kinney, Arthur F. "Tortilla Flat Re-Visited." In *John Steinbeck*, edited by Harold Bloom. New York: Chelsea House, 1987.

Parini, Jay. *John Steinbeck: A Biography.* New York: Henry Holt, 1995.

OF MICE AND MEN

Genre: Novel

Subgenre: Sentimental melodrama

Published: New York, 1937

Time period: 1930s

Setting: Central California's Salinas Valley

Themes and Issues. Steinbeck took this book's unusual title from a line in the Scottish poet Robert Burns's poem "To a Mouse": "The best laid schemes o' mice and men gang aft a-gley [astray]." This line hints at the central theme of the novel, which focuses on human dreams and shows how, for common Americans, they were derailed during the disillusionments of the Great Depression of the 1930s.

The central characters are Lennie Small, a mentally handicapped giant, and George Milton, his devoted friend. George has concocted his own tiny part of the American dream, which he repeatedly relates to Lennie. His dream is this: One day he and Lennie will live untroubled on their own farm, where they

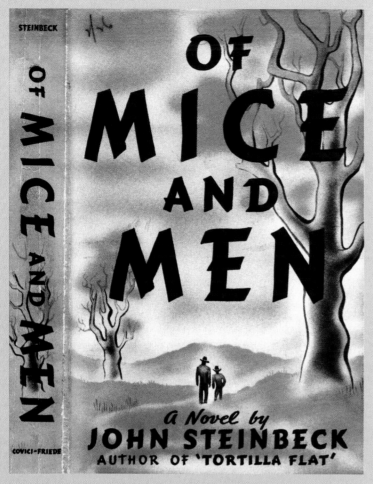

OF MICE AND MEN

A Novel by
JOHN STEINBECK
AUTHOR OF 'TORTILLA FLAT'

This old book cover for *Of Mice and Men* depicts the gentle giant Lennie walking off with his loyal friend and comrade George, forever in search of the American dream. Typical of Steinbeck stories, their hopes are dashed, and the tale is more about the journey than attainment.

will grow vegetables and raise chickens and rabbits that Lennie will feed.

The Plot. George and his friend Lennie are fleeing from a ranch where Lennie might have killed a woman he frightened, had George not knocked him out and taken him away. It is apparently not the first time George has saved Lennie from a would-be lynch mob.

The two friends hope for a fresh start with new jobs on a Salinas Valley ranch. George warns Lennie not to talk during their meeting with their new boss. He makes Lennie behave by reminding him of their dream of having a farm.

At the bunkhouse, the boss's unfriendly son, Curley, comes by to look them over. Candy, the bunkhouse maintenance man, then warns them that Curley is a dangerous hothead

jealously protective of his new wife. Lennie wants to leave immediately, but since he and George have no money, they must stay.

By evening Lennie is content in his childlike way, fondling a puppy another man has given him. Once again, he asks George to recite the dream about their farm. When Candy overhears the story, he tells George that he has saved $350, which he is willing to use to buy a farm all three men can share.

The future looks bright until Curley returns, looking for his wife. When he picks on Lennie, the giant refuses to fight but instead crushes Curley's hand in his own. While Curley goes to town for medical treatment, his wife visits Lennie in the bunkhouse. She is glad he has injured Curley.

Later, Lennie contentedly strokes his puppy, unaware that with his great strength he has accidentally killed it. Curley's wife then returns and asks Lennie to stroke her hair. When she tries to pull away, however, he holds her hair so tightly that she screams. Feeling panicked, Lennie shakes the woman violently to stop her screaming and accidentally breaks her neck. After he flees, Candy finds the woman's dead body, alerts George, and spreads the alarm. George gets a shotgun and joins the chase.

George finds Lennie crouching by the peaceful stream from which they drank earlier in the day. Expecting that the angry strangers will soon arrive and lynch Lennie, he recites the dream about the farm one last time, puts his gun to Lennie's head, and pulls the trigger.

Analysis. Steinbeck set *Of Mice and Men* in the region he knew best: the farmland of the Salinas Valley. Built around the theme of disillusionment, the story takes place during the Great Depression, when wage-paying jobs were scarce and the dream of ordinary ranch hands being able to buy their own land was merely that—a dream. Despite the story's strong topicality, it also treats the more universal themes of innocence and friendship.

Despite his immense size and strength, Lennie is a gentle innocent who wishes only to live in peace with his friend George and care for animals. His simple goals are unattainable, however, because the combination of his limited intelligence and superhuman strength repeatedly get him in trouble. Until the conclusion of the story, Lennie's steadfast friend George has always managed to rescue him from serious harm. After he accidentally kills the woman, George realizes that the only way he can now save George is by killing him himself, before the angry mob can abuse him. With the prospect of facing a murder charge, George rises to the highest level of heroism by risking his own life merely to spare his friend from humiliation.

This book is the best example of Steinbeck's skill in writing carefully crafted scenes. He wrote the book in a way that lent itself well to dramatic presentation. Shortly after the book's publication, a dramatic adaptation of its story opened on Broadway and met great success. In 1939 a film adaptation of the story was released, with Lon Chaney Jr., as Lennie and Burgess Meredith as George. Because of the way Steinbeck had written this book, the stage and film scripts were exceptionally faithful to the original story. New adaptations of the book were filmed in 1981 (for television) and in 1992.

SOURCES FOR FURTHER STUDY

Gannett, Lewis. "John Steinbeck: Novelist at Work." In *Conversations with John Steinbeck*, edited by Thomas Fensch. Jackson: University of Mississippi Press, 1988.

Hadella, Charlotte Cook. "The Dialogic Tension in Steinbeck's Portrait of Curley's Wife." *John Steinbeck: The Years of Greatness, 1936–1939*, edited by Tetsumaro Hayashi. Tuscaloosa: University of Alabama Press, 1993.

Johnson, Claudia D. *Understanding "Of Mice and Men," "The Red Pony," and "The Pearl": A Student Casebook to Issues, Sources, and Historical Documents.* Westport, Conn.: Greenwood Press, 1997.

Lewis, Cliff, and Carrol Britch, eds. *Rediscovering Steinbeck: Revisionist Views of His Art, Politics, and Intellect.* New York: Edward Mellen Press, 1989.

Marks, Lester Jay. *Thematic Design in the Novels of John Steinbeck.* The Hague: Mouton, 1969.

Morsberger, Robert E. "Tell Again, George." In *John Steinbeck: The Years of Greatness, 1936–1939*, edited by Tetsumaro Hayashi. Tuscaloosa: University of Alabama Press, 1993.

THE GRAPES OF WRATH

Genre: Novel
Subgenre: Social criticism
Published: New York, 1939
Time period: Mid-1930s
Setting: Overland journey from Oklahoma to California

Themes and Issues. In Steinbeck's great social protest novel, as in other works such as *Tortilla Flat* (1935), *The Red Pony* (1937), and *The Pearl* (1947), dreams that are achieved are dashed. The dream of the Joad family in *The Grapes of Wrath* is to find work and happiness in fertile California when they flee the dust bowl conditions of Oklahoma. After a long and difficult journey, they reach California, only to find new hardships and disenchantment. For the Joads—as for most dreamers in Steinbeck's fiction—there is no promised land.

The Grapes of Wrath also sustains two other strong themes throughout its story: the overwhelming importance of the family and the dignity of all human beings. The Joads survive their hardships by sticking together as a family. At the same time, they come to appreciate that thousands of other people share their hardships. By the end of the novel, they see their plight not only as a family struggle but also as a struggle to win dignity for all people. The novel thus concludes with the positive message of new hope superseding its message of disillusionment and despair.

The Plot. When Tom Joad returns to his Oklahoma home from prison for killing a man in self-defense, he finds his family preparing to move away. Longtime farmers, they are driven

The desperation of this Missouri family on Highway 99 in 1937, captured by the famed dust bowl photographer Dorothea Lange, mirrors the despair of the Joads, a family portraying the real lives of countless migrant workers in Steinbeck's Pulitzer Prize–winning classic *The Grapes of Wrath*.

Soon, the family has a brush with the law. When Tom is threatened with arrest, Jim Casy stands in for him and is arrested in his place. After leaving the first camp, they stop in a well-organized government camp. There, for the first time, they receive humane treatment. They also find work on nearby orchards, picking peaches for five cents a box. They earn enough money to buy food; however, to get to their jobs they must cross a picket line of workers striking for decent wages.

Jim Casy resurfaces as the leader of the strikers. In a scuffle with the law, he is killed, and Tom Joad is injured. Once again, the family must move on. They find refuge, along with other migrants, among abandoned boxcars. Still in danger of arrest, Tom leaves the family, promising to continue Casy's struggle for better working conditions.

Heavy rains transform a nearby stream into a torrent, flooding the boxcars, while Tom's sister, Rose of Sharon, delivers a stillborn baby. She swaddles the dead baby in cloth, and sets him adrift in the current. With their truck now useless, the remaining Joads leave the camp on foot and find shelter in a barn, where they meet a boy and his starving father. The story ends with Rose of Sharon offering her breast milk to the dying man.

Analysis. *The Grapes of Wrath* marked a turning point for Steinbeck as his most fully developed novel. He used it to move from the Arthurian influences found in his early work to a notable biblical influence. Biblical references include a veiled allusion to Jesus Christ in the martyred

from their home by the disastrous dust bowl conditions created by drought. Thirteen members of Tom's family and his friend Jim Casy crowd into the dilapidated truck that is to carry them across nearly two thousand miles of the arid Southwest to California. Leaflets they have read contain promises of abundant farmwork in the Golden State. Along their way, however, the Joads will meet people returning east who report that the leaflets lie.

On the first night out, Grampa Joad suffers a stroke and dies. Later Gramma Joad dies. Later the family truck breaks down, and merchants treat them badly. Despite these discouragements, the Joads still expect to find work in California. When they finally reach California, they stop in a crudely built migrant encampment, where they learn that work is unobtainable.

Jim Casy's initials ("J.C.") and an allusion to the baby Moses being set adrift in the bulrushes in Rose of Sharon's release of her stillborn baby.

Steinbeck also used this novel to perfect his use of interchapters to clarify some of the novel's philosophical impact. These sections, which are independent of the novel's narrative, discuss the broader situation in which the story takes place.

As a social document, *The Grapes of Wrath* presents such a vivid picture of oppression and misery that its very authenticity often seems in doubt. In writing the book, however, Steinbeck did more than academic research to gather information on migrant workers. He went from California to Oklahoma to observe conditions. He also worked alongside migrants and stayed in a migrant camp.

At the time of the book's original publication in 1939, much of its content was considered shocking. For example, Rose of Sharon's gesture in offering her breast milk to the dying man was controversial among both readers and critics. More widespread, however, were criticisms of the book's depiction of the harsh conditions among migrant farmworkers. Its depiction of the plight of migrant workers caused it to be regarded more as a social document than a mere work of fiction. Many readers saw the book as an exposé of capitalist excesses. Some even saw it as a call for revolution. The book was banned by many libraries and was publicly burned in parts of Oklahoma because of what Oklahomans considered its unfavorable depiction of their state and its people.

Although some readers of *The Grapes of Wrath* called the book's author a revolutionary, Steinbeck was basically a reformer. He sought not to overturn the free enterprise system but merely to change people's attitudes and behaviors. While he believed in calling attention to society's injustices, he had an underlying love for all human beings and a faith in the possibility of positive change. That faith emerges in the novel's symbolic acknowledgment that all people essentially belong together and are a part of a greater whole. *The Grapes of Wrath* can thus be read as an allegory for all people in all times.

Despite unfriendly reactions to the novel, it was awarded a Pulitzer Prize in 1940. When the book was adapted to the screen that same year, some of its starkness was softened. Nevertheless, the resulting film had an immense social impact of its own and helped to attract even more attention to the novel.

SOURCES FOR FURTHER STUDY

Bloom, Harold, ed. *John Steinbeck's "The Grapes of Wrath."* New York: Chelsea House, 1988.

Ditsky, John, ed. *Critical Essays on Steinbeck's "The Grapes of Wrath."* Boston: G. K. Hall, 1989.

Owens, Louis. *"The Grapes of Wrath": Trouble in the Promised Land.* New York: Twayne Publishers, 1989.

Shillinglaw, Susan, ed. *"The Grapes of Wrath:* A Special Issue." *San Jose Studies* 17 (Winter, 1990).

Wyatt, David, ed. *New Essays on "The Grapes of Wrath."* New York: Cambridge University Press, 1990.

Other Works

THE RED PONY (1937). In "The Gift," the first of three connected stories in this little book, Jody Tiflin is a farm boy coming of age in the Salinas Valley region of central California. His father buys him the red pony that he has long wanted, on the condition that he take proper care of it. As in much of Steinbeck's writing, a protagonist quests after something and eventually attains it.

Initially, Jody is overjoyed to have the pony. He depends on farmhand Billy Buck to teach him how to care for it. Ever well-meaning, Billy tells Jody one sunny day during the rainy season that he can leave his pony outdoors safely because it will not rain. Billy promises to put his pony in the stable if it does rain, but when rain comes, he forgets.

When the pony falls ill from being soaked,

Smith O'Brien's palette in the painting *The Cannery, 1931* tenders the warmth of the Cannery Row region in Monterey, California, a spot near and dear to Steinbeck's heart and pen, for he returned to this region again and again in his writing.

Billy promises it will be well the next morning. Again, he is wrong. The pony goes into a pasture and dies. When buzzards attack the fallen animal, Jody attempts to drive them off and kills one, but both his pony and his innocence are forever lost.

The book's other two stories, "The Great Mountains" and "The Promise," are also about disillusionment following attainment of quests. Both stories depict Jody Tiflin in various stages of development, often in some sort of rebellion against the disillusionment that comes with growing up and with the loss of innocence.

CANNERY ROW (1945). A novel without a plot, *Cannery Row* is about the diverse characters living on Cannery Row in the small fishing community of Monterey, California. The story unfolds like many of the Arthurian narratives in *Le Morte d'Arthur* as the characters organize a party to honor Doc, the proprietor of a biological supply company. The individual characters provide what structure the novel has. Each in his own way contributes to a full picture of

Cannery Row, as well as Doc, whom Steinbeck modeled on his friend Ed Ricketts.

The odd-numbered chapters in the book contain its central narrative. Several even-numbered chapters contain fables that present much of the novel's philosophy. These chapters do not relate directly to characters in the novel—a fact that has troubled many readers. The interchapters are puzzling and have been variously interpreted, but they focus largely on human isolation and on the need for people to be viewed favorably by those with whom they are closely associated.

Cannery Row offers a wonderfully warm depiction of the colorful characters who clustered around Monterey before it became a tourist mecca. The book was a commercial success because of its vivid descriptions of the area and the people in it, its flawless use of local color, and the warm humanity of Doc, the long-suffering, ever-forgiving recipient of a well-intentioned party that backfires.

THE PEARL (1947). *The Pearl* was one of Steinbeck's more popular stories with the reading public but was not well regarded by critics. It focuses on a simple peasant man, about whom Steinbeck had heard while he was in Mexico during the early 1940s. A young, newly married pearl diver, Kino finds an oyster containing what he calls "the pearl of the world"—the largest ever found in his vicinity.

Until his great find, Kino is treated with indifference, even contempt. For example, when his son is made sick by a scorpion sting, the pompous village doctor refuses to treat the boy because Kino has no money. After Kino becomes a celebrity, his life changes. Villagers, including the unfeeling doctor, flock around him hoping to share his good fortune.

Later, however, pearl merchants try to cheat Kino, fellow villagers try to steal his pearl, and disillusionment sets in. Disenchanted by the hypocrisy of those around him, Kino finally throws his magnificent pearl back into the sea. He concludes that it will bring him nothing but pain and mistrust.

EAST OF EDEN (1952). Steinbeck wrote *East of Eden* as a personal testament for his sons. The novel was intended to present the record of his own forebears' coming to the Salinas Valley from the East after the Civil War. It has strong autobiographical elements and is largely about Steinbeck's mother's family, the Hamiltons. Originally intended to be a first-person account, it became a third-person account with occasional lapses into the first-person.

The story begins with Adam Trask marrying Cathy Ames in Connecticut and settling in California. There his wife later abandons him and their twin sons, Caleb and Aron, and becomes the keeper of a notorious brothel. A major figure in the book, she knows more about the respectable members of the community than anyone else. She is determined to have her way and has no scruples about destroying anyone standing between her and what she wants.

Cathy finally is compromised by her assistant Joe, a character whom Steinbeck forgives by pointing out the difficulties of his childhood. Realizing that she can probably outwit Joe, Cathy knows, nevertheless, that in the end someone will come along who will defeat her, a fate she cannot bear to contemplate. She commits suicide, but her suicide is inconsistent with her character as Steinbeck presents her.

The motion picture adapted from *East of Eden* in 1955 launched James Dean's brief but spectacular acting career. Largely because of the teenage audiences's attraction to Dean, the film was a commercial success, even though the novel was disappointing.

Resources

Major collections of John Steinbeck manuscripts can be found at such institutions as University of Virginia, University of Texas at Austin, New York Public Library, Columbia University Library, and Stanford University Library. Other institutions and organizations of interest to students of John Steinbeck include the following:

Cannery Row Foundation. An organization in Monterey, California, that promotes tourism, the foundation honors Steinbeck's memory and maintains a useful Web site (http://www.canneryrow.org).

International John Steinbeck Society. Based in Muncie, Indiana, this organization is dedicated to the study of Steinbeck and publishes the *Steinbeck Quarterly*.

John Steinbeck Project. Based at Southampton College of Long Island University—near Steinbeck's last residence—this project honors John Steinbeck's memory by fostering special programs for visiting writers, an annual lecture series, student writing awards, and special scholarships. (http://www.southampton.liunet.edu)

National Steinbeck Center. A modern museum facility in Salinas, California, this center has a major collection of Steinbeck materials, including "Rocinante," the truck he drove across the country with his dog, Charley. The center's Web site offers voluminous information and pictures that relate to Steinbeck's life and work, as well as links to other Steinbeck sites. (http://www.steinbeck.org)

San Jose State University Steinbeck Research Center. Founded in 1971, this center has one of the world's top Steinbeck archives, with more than 10,000 manuscripts, original letters, inscribed first editions, secondary works, film memorabilia, photographs, films, and cassettes. The center publishes the biannual *Steinbeck Newsletter* and maintains an exceptionally valuable Web site: (http://www.sjsu.edu/depts/steinbec/frchome.html).

R. BAIRD SHUMAN

Wallace Stevens

BORN: October 2, 1879, Reading, Pennsylvania
DIED: August 2, 1955, Hartford, Connecticut
IDENTIFICATION: Mid-twentieth-century poet known for his powerful poems on the relationship between the imagination and reality and for his energetic attempts to create a poetry appropriate to his time.

Wallace Stevens's first book *Harmonium* (1923) startled the literary world with its wit, its complexity, and its sheer joy in wordplay—what a reviewer called its "dandyism." Stevens's later works went on to develop a sophisticated idea of poetry that gave poetry the same weight as religion, carrying terms and symbols from one to the other. Stevens has been seen as a spokesman for various religious and philosophical ideas, including those of atheism, Buddhism, and Christianity. The philosophical content of Stevens's work, combined with its literary value, has given it a broad appeal to others besides readers of poetry. He is quoted in books on history and physics as well as by philosophers and writers worldwide.

Wallace Stevens was born on October 2, 1879, to Garrett Stevens, a lawyer, and his wife, Margarethe Zeller Stevens. His mother's religious faith and lively imagination and his father's preoccupation with earning money made an early mark on the young Stevens. Stevens gave evidence from childhood of a love of words, expressed, for example, in his playful, clever letters home from camp, but he was raised to believe that the primary goal of a young man was to earn a respectable living.

Childhood. Stevens's childhood with his two sisters and two brothers in relatively comfortable circumstances allowed him the freedom to explore nature. His childhood letters and journals show the vast knowledge he acquired on long walks in the country around his home in Reading, Pennsylvania.

As an adolescent Stevens was pulled in two directions, toward literature and toward law. When he enrolled at Harvard University in 1897, he intended to follow his father's ambition for him to become a lawyer. However, he also loved to write. He published his first work, Victorian in style, in *The Harvard Advocate*. At the same time, however, he was learning and expanding his horizons with the best literary and philosophical minds of the time, such as Irving Babbitt and George Santayana. Stevens left the school in 1900 when financial problems crippled his father's law practice. At this time, he decided to become a reporter and went to New York City.

Youth. In New York Stevens attempted to support himself as reporter for the *New York Herald Tribune* and as an editorial assistant for *World's Work,* a monthly magazine, while doing freelance work on the side. However, he was unable to support himself in what he considered comfort so he enrolled in the law school at New York University in 1901.

In 1904 he was admitted to the bar in New York. That same year, on a visit home to Reading, he met Elsie Viola Moll, the outstandingly lovely woman whose profile was the model for the Liberty Head dime

Although Stevens's parents nurtured his love of reading, his traditional upbringing left little room for the literary aspirations of a young poet.

Nature was a powerful influence on the early work of the poet. Stevens loved to walk, all the time amassing his keen observations.

and the Walking Liberty half-dollar. In love with Elsie and wanting to marry her, Stevens was mindful of his father's advice and example; he put off marriage for some years until he felt he could support a wife and family.

Stevens began practicing law in New York—working briefly for several law firms—and saving to marry. He continued writing and composed poems to Elsie that he presented to her in two small handmade books, "A Book of Verse" and "The Little June Book." Although these poems are bland and traditional, Stevens was during this time associating with and learning from the poets, writers, and artists who formed the exciting New York literary scene.

Despite the fact that some of them were destroyed, the many detailed and loving letters Stevens sent to Elsie during their long engagement show his development as a poet. The long-awaited marriage took place in 1909, and the young couple set up housekeeping in New York, where Stevens worked for the American Bonding Company as a lawyer.

Stevens's father disapproved of his choice of a bride, and the two men were never recon-ciled. The deaths of both his parents took place in the following three years. Stevens's first poetry to appear after these major life events was vastly different in both style and content than his previous poetry. His first mature poems were published as "Carnet de Voyage" in *Trend* in 1914, and in contrast to the melodic outbursts of "The Little June Book," these new poems were learned, complex, and deliberately off-key.

While Stevens worked hard to establish himself as an insurance lawyer, he also was intoxicated by the New York art world of the 1910s. He was intrigued by experimental artists such as the Dadaists, who poked fun of traditional art in startling ways, such as elevating a urinal to art by creating an artist for it and signing it. He also favored the futurists, who were in love with the mechanical and tried to capture the motion of the new machines on canvas. Artists and writers met in private homes to discuss the new art movements, and Stevens joined them when he could. Stevens's involvement with the art world at least partly influenced the poems of his first published collection, *Harmonium* (1923). Another formative influence was a business trip to Florida, which so impressed Stevens that its images dominate his first book.

Midlife. Stevens succeeded in both the literary and the business worlds, but it was not long before he found his marriage to be less than successful. After the birth of the couple's only daughter, Holly Bright Stevens, in 1924, Elsie's beauty faded rapidly, and she began wearing dowdy, unattractive clothes. It also became clear that her interests did not match those of her husband. Elsie tended as she grew older to become more reclusive, primarily interested in her household and garden. Stevens, in contrast, escaped into poetry and the world of ideas and images. He and his wife eventually shared little more than their daughter and, later, an interest in genealogy.

Because Stevens lived so intensely the life of the mind, there are few noteworthy events in his life. In 1916 he had joined the Hartford Accident and Indemnity Company, and he rose through the ranks of the organization through hard work, conscientiousness, and business ability. He wrote books of poetry and gave readings, although he was never comfortable as a reader and this stiffness of manner comes through in the recordings that have been preserved. His books gained an increasingly larger following over the years. Stevens did not travel much after he became vice president of the Hartford Accident and Indemnity Company in 1934 and did not have to travel to settle claims. He did not vacation abroad, preferring the images of distant places in his head to the realities of foreign tourism. He sometimes had friends who were going overseas bring him back well-chosen souvenirs, which in his mind were representative of the places from which they came. The vivid daring of his poems contrasts strongly with the rigid regularity of his life.

Old Age. Stevens's books appeared at satisfying intervals: *Ideas of Order* in 1935, *The Man with the Blue Guitar and Other Poems* in 1937, *Parts of a World* in 1942, and *Transport to Summer* in 1947. Stevens himself was showered with honors, including the prestigious Yale University Bollingen Prize in Poetry for 1949, and many honorary degrees. He won the National Book Award twice, and was given the Pulitzer Prize just before his death. His last two books were *The Auroras of Autumn* (1950) and *The Collected Poems of Wallace Stevens* (1954). During the last years of his life he became preoccupied anew with the issue of transcendence, or the question of whether there is a God. His last poems explore the meaning of a single life, particularly a poet's life, as seen from its very end. They also examine the possibility of the existence of a creator and try to define such a creator. Stevens died of cancer on August 2, 1955, after converting to Roman Catholicism on his deathbed.

Stevens's continued success as an insurance lawyer brought the family to Hartford, Connecticut. Here, he stands outside the family home at 118 Westerly Terrace.

HIGHLIGHTS IN STEVENS'S LIFE

1879	Wallace Stevens is born on October 2 in Reading, Pennsylvania.
1897	Enrolls at Harvard University.
1900	Moves to New York to be a journalist.
1901	Attends law school at New York University.
1903	Graduates from law school.
1904	Is admitted to New York state bar; meets Elsie Viola Moll.
1905	Begins working for a series of New York law firms.
1908	Joins American Bonding Company; writes "A Book of Verses," a collection of poems for Elsie's birthday.
1909	Writes "The Little June Book," a collection of poems for Elsie's birthday; marries Elsie and settles in New York.
1911	Father dies.
1912	Mother dies.
1914	Stevens publishes "Carnet de Voyage," a set of eight poems, in Trend.
1916	Joins Hartford Accident and Indemnity Company; moves permanently to Connecticut.
1920	Wins Poetry magazine prize.
1923	Publishes *Harmonium,* his first poetry collection.
1924	Daughter, Holly Bright, is born.
1932	Stevens moves family to 188 Westerly Terrace, in Hartford.
1935	Publishes *Ideas of Order* with Alcestis Press; it is reissued by Knopf the following year.
1937	Publishes *The Man with the Blue Guitar and Other Poems.*
1942	Publishes *Parts of a World.*
1945	Publishes *Esthétique du Mal.*
1946	Is inducted into the National Institute of Arts and Letters.
1947	Publishes *Transport to Summer.*
1949	Is awarded Bollingen Prize in Poetry.
1950	Publishes *The Auroras of Autumn,* which wins National Book Award.
1951	Publishes *The Necessary Angel: Essays on Reality and the Imagination.*
1954	Publishes *The Collected Poems of Wallace Stevens,* which receives National Book Award and Pulitzer Prize.
1955	Dies on August 2 in Hartford, Connecticut, after converting to Roman Catholicism.
1957	*Opus Posthumous* is published posthumously.
1966	*Letters of Wallace Stevens,* edited by Holly Stevens, is published.

Wallace Stevens is known for his poetry. The few unsuccessful plays he wrote as a young man are now interesting mainly for what they show about his poetry. Stevens's essays are all attempts to clarify his views on what kind of poetry should be written and why poetry is important, even in times of trouble.

Belief in the Power of Poetry. Although as a young man Stevens wrote plays, and as a journalist he also wrote articles, he devoted his intellectual life mainly to poetry. He believed in poetry as a powerful force for social as well as intellectual progress, once saying in a speech that poetry's function was "to help men live their lives." Even though he admired and loved his mother, he could no longer as an adult accept the faith that she had tried to instill into her young children by reading them Bible stories and teaching them prayers. He held the idea that poetry could take the place of religion as a force for good, with poets as priests.

The Absence of God. Part of the theme of Steven's first book is that the childhood God no

Suffused in greens, Georges Lemmers's *After Tea* (Galerie Berko, Brussels, Belgium) reflects the quiet contemplation of such poems as "Sunday Morning."

longer is active in the world, and it is important to find something to take its place. The first God-substitute Stevens discovers is joy in nature. He suggests that people take pleasure in natural things such as sunlight, trees, flowers, and fruit, instead of going to worship in churches and pondering the afterlife. For instance, in "Sunday Morning" he presents a woman, perhaps an imagined version of his mother, who is concerned about religion, death, and immortality. He provides another voice, perhaps the poet's own, arguing with her that the world provides good things that she can love as much as the idea of Heaven.

Abbott Handerson Thayer's oil painting *Sky Simulated by Red Flamingoes* (Smithsonian American Art Museum, Washington, D.C.) points to the vibrant and lush world Stevens discovered on his trip to Florida. The state proved to be a place to which Stevens could imaginatively respond in his work.

Stevens's Symbolism.
In Stevens's early poetry, everything in the world is divided into opposing pairs—day and night, man and woman, sun and moon, reality and imagination. Stevens uses colors as symbols: blue, for instance, stands for the imagination, and green for reality. Some of his nature symbols are mostly common sense: Dew, for instance, because it evaporates, suggests the fact that life changes and ends. A flickering flame on a candle stands for human awareness or consciousness. In Stevens's later poems the symbols become complicated and have many levels of interpretation.

Imagination and Reality.
Stevens was also concerned with the relationship between the imagination and reality. Human beings were most godlike to Stevens in their ability to imagine or to create. However, it was important that creation not stray too far from reality; if it did, it was empty. It was the poet's responsibility to represent reality as seen through the imagination, not simply to invent things. Much of Stevens's first book was stimulated by his trip to Florida, and its themes and images often evoke that southern state.

Development.
Stevens's work changed as he grew older, reflecting his changing philosophy. Most readers new to Stevens read the poems in his first book or two, which are easier to understand; as he grew older he incorporated ideas from philosophers and critics, making his works dense with meaning. His first book, *Harmonium,* is mostly about the imagination and reality, and its colorful images of Florida show the imagination at work on the real. His second work, *Ideas of Order,* for the most part rejects Florida as a subject

Pablo Picasso's 1909 painting *Factory at Horta de Ebro*. Picasso's modernist renderings influenced Stevens, and there is a noted affinity between both men's work with their varied perspectives and new ways of looking at the conventional and everyday.

and chooses to talk about human beings in society instead of nature.

Stevens's notion of the poet as a powerful figure whose right and duty it is to be the spokesperson of his time emerges in *The Man with the Blue Guitar and Other Poems*. This book consists mostly of one poem that is based partly on Picasso's picture of an old guitarist. The poem discusses what it means to be an artist in difficult times. Later works take the figure of the poet even further, making him godlike in his ability to see to the heart of the world he lives in, to describe it, and to preserve it.

Later Work. Stevens's last work takes up ideas of God, and explores what they might mean. Some theologians do not have a concept of a God that always stays the same, but consider that God evolves just as creation does. Some of

Stevens's forays into religious thinking present such an evolving God. Some of Stevens's late poems are extremely complicated, allowing very different interpretations. The difficulty of his later work is caused by his ambiguous use of grammar, where specific sentences could mean different things; by his use of words with multiple meanings; and by the extreme complexity of his thought. However, readers who have followed Stevens throughout the course of his development will find it worthwhile to try to unravel these final poems, such as "The Rock."

Stevens's Literary Legacy. Stevens was concerned with saving poetry as a social force at a time when chaos appeared to have taken over society. His whole intellectual life was devoted to defining poetry as a positive influence and to attempting to write poetry that explained his views by showing how they worked. He wrote poetry about writing poetry and about how poets should relate to the world in which they live and which they describe.

Stevens arguably may be the most influential of the modernist poets. The modernists wrote mostly between World War I and World War II. Because their world of certainty had been shattered by World War I, then called "the Great War," they represented the disruption of the social order in their poems. Other modernist poets included Ezra Pound, T. S. Eliot, and Marianne Moore. Often they wrote about a search for values in a society that had discarded or abandoned its old values. Stevens's intense search for poetic truth and the way he defined poetry as a positive social value left its mark on other poets. His lyrical style also demonstrated that it was possible for poetry to be exalted even in the twentieth century.

BIBLIOGRAPHY

Baird, James. *The Dome and the Rock: Structure in the Poetry of Wallace Stevens.* Baltimore: John Hopkins University Press, 1968.

Bates, Milton J. *Wallace Stevens: A Mythology of Self.* Berkeley: University of California Press, 1985.

Brazeau, Peter. *Parts of a World: Wallace Stevens Remembered, An Oral Biography.* New York: Random House, 1983.

Carroll, Joseph. *Wallace Stevens's Supreme Fiction: A New Romanticism.* Baton Rouge: Louisiana State University Press, 1987.

Filreis, Alan. *Wallace Stevens and the Actual World.* Princeton, N.J.: Princeton University Press, 1991.

Fisher, Barbara M. *Wallace Stevens: The Intensest Rendezvous.* Charlottesville: University Press of Virginia, 1991.

Kermode, Frank. *Wallace Stevens.* New York: Grove Press, 1961.

McCann, Janet. *Wallace Stevens Revisited: The Celestial Possible.* New York: Twayne Publishers/Simon and Schuster, 1995.

O'Connor, William Van. *The Shaping Spirit: A Study of Wallace Stevens.* New York: Russell and Russell, 1964.

Penso, Kio. *Wallace Stevens, "Harmonium," and the Whole of Harmonium.* New York: Archon Books, 1991.

Richardson, Joan. *Wallace Stevens.* 2 vols. New York: Beech Tree Books, 1986, 1988.

Riddel, Joseph N. *The Clairvoyant Eye: The Poetry and Poetics of Wallace Stevens.* Baton Rouge: Louisiana State University Press, 1965.

Stevens, Holly. *Souvenirs and Prophecies: The Young Wallace Stevens.* New York: Knopf, 1977.

POETRY

1923 Harmonium (with fourteen additional poems, 1931)
1935 Ideas of Order
1936 Owl's Clover
1937 The Man with the Blue Guitar and Other Poems
1942 Parts of a World
1942 Notes Toward a Supreme Fiction
1945 Description Without Place
1945 Esthétique du Mal
1947 Transport to Summer
1950 The Auroras of Autumn
1953 Selected Poems
1954 The Collected Poems of Wallace Stevens

NONFICTION

1947 Three Academic Pieces
1951 The Necessary Angel: Essays on Reality and the Imagination
1966 Letters of Wallace Stevens, ed. Holly Stevens
1977 Souvenirs and Prophecies: The Young Wallace Stevens

MISCELLANEOUS

1957 Opus Posthumous, ed. Samuel French Morse

PLAYS

1916 Three Travelers Watch a Sunrise
1917 Carlos Among the Candles
1917 Bowl, Cat, and Broomstick

Wallace Stevens's Conversion to Roman Catholicism

Wallace Stevens's death from stomach cancer was preceded by a period of limited activity. Frequently plagued by intestinal problems, he initially assumed that his discomfort was just a matter of getting old. He finally was persuaded to have an exploratory operation and was diagnosed with terminal cancer. He was never told of the cancer, as was often the case in the time period, but was told instead that he had a serious stomach illness from which he would recover. He must, however, have known otherwise, and his last few months were marked by an intense religious interest and study. Prior to his final illness, he had shown an interest in religion, particularly Roman Catholicism, and had religious material sent to his office, so that his family would not see it.

Baptism. During Stevens's final hospitalization in 1955, he joined the Roman Catholic church. He had spoken about his growing interest in Roman Catholicism with sympathetic friends and finally asked Father Arthur Hanley, who was acting as hospital chaplain, to take him into the Church by means of baptism. Stevens had several study periods with Father Hanley before the baptism, but in fact he had been thinking about this act for some time. He told Father Hanley he intended to write Roman Catholic poems if he lived; poems to celebrate and to affirm the Church. He did not live to write these poems but died shortly after the baptism.

Relevance. There is a large gap between the positions Stevens explored in his final poems, which discuss God but not Christ, and his acceptance of the Roman Catholic Church. In his last poems, such as "Presence of an External Master of Knowledge," Stevens explores the idea of God and sets forth a concept of God as a kind of divine imaginer. The poems are intellectual philosophical explorations, rather than expressions of personal commitment. The final step was a leap of faith. Stevens scholars were not generally happy when it leaked out in the 1970s that his conversion had taken place. Some denied it, and some trivialized it. However, Stevens had spoken of his growing pull toward Catholicism with all his Catholic friends. He had spoken of his spiritual neediness to Father Cassian Yuhaus, Father Hanley, the nurses in the hospital, and others. When he decided to commit, he asked Father Hanley to bring him into the Church through bap-

In a July 24, 1977, letter to Professor Janet McCann, Father Arthur Hanley wrote of Stevens's alleged conversion, "The first time he came to the hospital, he expressed a certain emptiness in his life. . . . At least three times, he talked about getting into the fold—meaning the Catholic Church. He often remarked about the peace and tranquillity that he experienced in going into a Catholic Church and spending some time. He spoke about St. Patrick's Cathedral in New York." The photograph shows a procession of clergy at the famous cathedral.

tism and Father Hanley did. No one was told then; but after his death, Father Hanley and the Catholic friends spoke to others, and the matter became public some years later. Although Stevens died in 1955, the conversion was not known generally until the mid-1970s.

General Disbelief. It was difficult for some to believe that Stevens would take the final step toward conversion at a time when Roman Catholicism was somewhat negatively perceived. This disbelief came from two sources: the fact that Holly Stevens, Stevens's daughter, denied that the conversion took place, and the fact that Father Hanley did not file any baptismal certificate. However, not only did Father Hanley confirm the events, but also others associated with Stevens during his final illness spoke of his intense interest in Roman Catholicism. Moreover, Father Hanley was notoriously casual with paperwork. As for Holly Stevens, she was known to be anti-Catholic, and her father would not have discussed his conversion with her for fear of upsetting her. There seems little doubt that the deathbed baptism occurred; what it means is another matter.

Meaning. Some critics believe that since Stevens was an insurance executive, he was merely taking out one final policy. Others suggest that because he was in a Roman Catholic hospital, he was under pressure from the nuns to join the Church. However, such conversions were very unusual, and in fact Stevens's baptism had been preceded by years of reading and of conversations about theology. The direction may have begun when Stevens as a young man in New York would to go into Saint Patrick's Cathedral to meditate. As early as 1902 he wrote in his journal, "Last night I spent an hour in the dark transept of St. Patrick's Cathedral where I go now and then in my more lonely moods." Even when he was a skeptic, he gained some comfort from the church. Over the course of his life he kept up a correspondence with a scholar nun, Sister Bernetta Quinn; his letters suggest that he admired the steadfast quality of her faith, although at that time he could not bring himself to share it.

Since Stevens has been thought of as the poet who rejected Christianity in favor of a celebration of the world, his final choice is noteworthy. His early poems mourned the loss of religion in his life. He later tried various substitutes for his childhood Protestantism, including poetry, Buddhism, and a kind of philosophy. He finally was moved to reaccept Christianity. While this final choice does not mean that all his poems should be reinterpreted as Christian poems, it does suggest that the search for ultimate truth that underlies all his work is of major importance in understanding Stevens.

SOURCES FOR FURTHER STUDY

Carroll, Joseph. *Wallace Stevens's Supreme Fiction: A New Romanticism.* Baton Rouge: Louisiana State University Press, 1987.

McCann, Janet. *Wallace Stevens Revisited: The Celestial Possible.* New York: Twayne Publishers/Simon & Schuster, 1995.

Peter Sickles's *Bustling City* suggests the marked change in Stevens's work as he grew older. In his later volumes, the poems become densely layered, more complex renderings of the spiritual implications of modern life.

Reader's Guide to Major Works

HARMONIUM

Genre: Poetry
Subgenre: Romanticism
Published: New York, 1923
Time period: Timeless present
Setting: Various settings

Themes and Issues. For many readers, their entire experience of Stevens will be this glittering, witty collection. Most of Stevens's commonly anthologized poems, including "The Emperor of Ice-Cream," "Sunday Morning," and "Anecdote of the Jar," are found in this volume. A harmonium was a musical instrument popular in homes in Stevens's youth, and these poems may be seen to represent various chords; they frequently refer to music.

Many of these poems are set in Florida, and they use the lush sensual images of the South in their attempts to find a balance between imagination and reality. Stevens wanted poetry to be both imagined and real. He disliked the romantic elaborations of some poets who went before him, believing that merely to invent things and to create beings falsified the world and therefore did not adequately represent it. At the same time, he believed that poetry should not be like a photograph, merely a simple description of what was there; this kind of poetry would be too miscellaneous and pointless. Stevens wanted to find the right balance of interpretation and simple sight to make poetry.

Stevens's "Anecdote of a Jar" begins, "I placed a jar in Tennessee, and round it was upon a hill." In this well-known poem, the poet describes how the wilderness and our perception of it are changed merely by adding a human-made object. These tire tracks in the snow suggest the same sort of presence.

Another important, and related, theme in Stevens's work is the rejection of Christianity. As a young man, Stevens saw Christianity as an invention such as the imaginings of overly romantic poets. He also saw religion as barring the way to true experience of this world, which he held as a goal. In such poems as "A High-Toned Old Christian Woman," he compares what he thought of as the stiff, forbidding Christian approach to life with a more high-spirited alternative.

Also akin to Stevens's imagination-reality balance was a focus on the vitality of nature. If religion and other idea-based approaches to life falsified poetry, then immersion in nature helped make it true. His vivid images of the South help clarify his position.

The Poems. Although most of the poems in *Harmonium* have been discussed by literary critics, three stand out as most frequently reprinted in anthologies and basic textbooks. These are "Sunday Morning," "The Emperor of Ice-Cream," and "Anecdote of the Jar."

"Sunday Morning" describes Stevens's rejection of his childhood religion and looks toward nature-worship as a replacement. The poem begins with a woman who is enjoying Sunday morning with coffee and oranges and is not going to church. The woman feels guilty about taking pleasure in worldly things and not following religious traditions. Another voice in the poem, perhaps the poet's, tells her she should enjoy the earth and not concern herself with the afterlife. She says that she does enjoy nature but asks about death. The voice answers that the earth has a kind of immortality, with its seasonal renewal, and that an imagined afterlife would be dull. "Death is the mother of beauty," he says, meaning in part that people value things because they pass away. The voice suggests that people should worship nature, which would include humanity itself, in the natural setting of which it is part. At the end of the poem, the woman seems to accept the position that she should embrace the world.

This poem is written in blank verse, which means that each of its lines contain five stressed syllables preceded by five unstressed syllables. This form adds dignity to the argument.

"The Emperor of Ice-Cream" is like "Sunday Morning" in its emphasis on the present. The funeral of a woman is described. She was a poor woman; she had cheap furniture, but she tried to add color to her life by embroidering her linens. She is dead now, the poem says, and life remains with the living—the people who roll cigars, the people who make ice cream. The poem ends, "The only emperor is the emperor of ice-cream." Ice cream is a good symbol for passing pleasures because it melts. An ice-cream company executive once wrote to Stevens asking whether his poem was for ice cream or against it. According to the poem, people should acknowledge—pay homage to—the truth that change rules the world. This poem too suggests that people live in the moment and not in the hope of some other world.

"Anecdote of the Jar" is a difficult poem that is often anthologized, even though there is no agreement on its meaning. The poem begins with the line, "I placed a jar in Tennessee," and then goes on to describe how the placement of the jar changed the landscape—the jar becomes the focus of the landscape, and the wildness of the landscape orders itself around the jar. The main characteristic of the jar is that it is different, "it did not give of bird or bush." Some readers see the jar as art, but if it is art, its ordering of nature does not seem to be a good one. It is possible to see the jar as any human intervention in the landscape, anything that interrupts the natural with the human.

"Anecdote of the Jar" is interesting partly because there is no clear and single meaning. It is open to a variety of readings, like much of late twentieth-century poetry.

Analysis. Stevens's first book received mixed reviews. Readers of the time were used to clarity; Stevens was a master of indirectness. In addition, the poetry's message, when it did come through clearly, was not popular. Some critics found Stevens's work overly complicated and obscure. However, other critics saw how strikingly different this poetry was, and they acknowledged that Stevens's wordplay, his images, and his unusual use of traditional forms would be recognized in the future.

Stevens's view of religion changed greatly over the course of his writing career, but most readers are most familiar with *Harmonium's*, negative views of traditional Christianity.

SOURCES FOR FURTHER STUDY

Burney, William A. *Wallace Stevens.* New York: Twayne Publishers, 1969.

MacLeod, Glen. *Wallace Stevens and Company: The "Harmonium" Years.* Ann Arbor, Mich.: UMI Research Press, 1985.

Rehder, Robert. *The Poetry of Wallace Stevens.* New York: St. Martin's Press, 1988.

Vendler, Helen. *Words Chosen out of Desire.* Knoxville: University of Tennessee Press, 1984.

IDEAS OF ORDER

Genre: Poetry collection
Subgenre: Realism
Published: New York, 1935
Time period: Timeless present
Setting: Various locations

Themes and Issues. Stevens waited a long time before issuing his second collection, no doubt partly because his work at the insurance company and his daughter, Holly, born in 1924, required his full attention. He commented in letters about how little time he had to write during this period. Nevertheless when he did release his second major collection, more than twelve years after the first, it was immediately clear that the direction and style of his work had changed dramatically.

Stevens banished from his book and his poetic palette the lush images of Florida that give the earlier poems their color and life. He was most concerned at this time with justifying poetry in times of trouble. He wanted to write about the lives of men, "men in crowds," rather than the beauty of the natural world. He decided that the poet could not escape from the world, even into nature. Many of these poems express sadness that one cannot escape into nature, but must live in and write poetry about the world of society, even though that world was in a state of breakdown. A number of these poems seem like good-bye poems—the poet is saying good-bye to a world that once was, a world in which poetry played a vital part. Some of these titles indicate Stevens's state of mind: "Waving Adieu, Adieu, Adieu," "A Fading of the Sun," "Sad Strains of a Gay Waltz," "Autumn Refrain." Instead of the blues, greens, reds, and golds of *Harmonium,* dark colors and minor keys are found throughout this book.

The Poems. Two poems from this collection that are found in many twentieth-century anthologies are "The Idea of Order at Key West" and "Farewell to Florida." Both of these poems stress the new direction of Stevens's poetry.

"Farewell to Florida," the first poem of the collection, expresses that the poet no longer thinks, if he ever did, that the mind should simply yield to reality in creating poetry. Florida's lushness suggests this relationship between the mind and the world—that the vivid landscape is in charge, and the mind is its slave. The poem comments that "The snake has left its skin upon the floor," meaning that a transformation is taking place, as snakes shed their old skins and then develop new ones.

The person speaking in the poem is on a ship and begins by saying, "Go on, high ship . . ." telling the ship to leave behind the South, with its dead images, and go toward the North, where there is action instead of the passive and deathlike beauty of the South. The speaker has chosen to go north and engage with difficult human issues instead of enjoying the natural beauty that the woman of "Sunday Morning," in Stevens's first collection, is urged to enjoy. The North will bring him "a slime of men in crowds," not the loveliness of Florida's blooms. He says he will not look back but will pass willingly from warmth to coldness, from relaxed nature to the "violent mind" of men. He desires to put romanticism behind him and be-

Stevens's book *Ideas of Order* adopts a slightly grim, more renunciatory vision. Edvard Munch's *Il Ballo della Vita (The Dance of Life)* suggests the blending of connection and distance present in Stevens's "Sad Strains of a Gay Waltz."

come a poet of the real, even though the real is not beautiful.

"The Idea of Order at Key West" does take images of the South, but it is not looking at the South itself. Rather it looks at what poetry does to nature. The poem speaks of how a woman sings about the sea and the differences between her song of the sea and the sounds the sea makes. The sea needs the woman's song to be understood by human beings, even though she has to change its language into human language to sing it. Afterward, the man who listened to the woman's song speaks of another man, a friend and fellow listener, and asks him to explain how her song of the sea managed to change how the harbor looked to him. That is, because she sang of it, its appearance was changed for him. The poem ends suggesting that art is a "blessed rage for order;" people need art to make sense of and to enrich their experiences.

Analysis. Stevens's book did not meet universal acclaim, although it was more widely reviewed and noted than his first book. Critics recognized Stevens's great ability, but some felt that Stevens should be more in tune with the times—which is ironic, because that is exactly what he attempts in this collection. Later critics focused on these poems as masterpieces of intellectual depth and artistic insight. The poems show Stevens's attempts to present poetry as a serious enterprise with far-reaching social results, as opposed to ornament and wordplay intended mainly to please.

SOURCES FOR FURTHER STUDY

Axelrod, Steven Gould, and Helen Deese, eds. *Critical Essays on Wallace Stevens.* Boston: G. K. Hall, 1988.

Kessler, Edward. *Images of Wallace Stevens.* New Brunswick, N.J.: Rutgers University Press, 1971.

Rehder, Robert. *The Poetry of Wallace Stevens.* New York: St. Martin's Press, 1988.

SOME INSPIRATIONS BEHIND STEVENS'S WORK

Wallace Stevens was greatly inspired by his mother, whose lively imagination and religious stories helped turn him toward poetry. He was also influenced by his father's warnings about making a living. He desired to do both things—make a good living and create art—and he did. His childhood hikes around the countryside of Reading, Pennsylvania, increased his knowledge and love of nature. His family influence also included the fact that he was of Pennsylvania Dutch ancestry, and Stevens used ancestral figures in his poems.

The American involvement in World War I, in which his youngest sister was killed, focused Stevens's attention on the waste of war. The later upheaval of World War II was also influential to his work.

The art groups in New York, with whom Stevens associated just after his marriage, gave him a taste for the experimental in his work and a knowledge of the new art movements that were rapidly changing the concept of art. Other influences include readings of Dante's medieval epic of heaven and hell, *La divina commedia* (ca. 1320; Eng. trans. *The Divine Comedy*, 1802; 3 vols.), and of many art and literary critics.

Stevens's travels during his early adulthood, especially his business trip to Florida, provided him with the strong and colorful images in his early work.

Stevens's later friendships and correspondence with people in distant places, such as the Cuban poet José Rodríguez Feo, replenished his work with new images. Stevens's strong sense of place was nourished more often by hearing about places and having personal friends in those locations than by visiting them himself.

Jean Metzinger's *Colorful Landscape with Aquatic Birds* suggests the lush and vivid tapestry of Florida, which presented itself to Stevens as a setting rife with poetic and imaginative possibilities.

Other Works

THE AURORAS OF AUTUMN (1950). Stevens's next to last major poetry collection begins again to look at the issue of religion and to imagine the qualities of God. At this time Stevens was looking back on the life he had lived as a poet. He asks in these poems what a poet's lifetime output ultimately means. Because he always focused on the imagination, he entertained the idea of a God as a kind of overwhelming imagination, who creates the individual flickers that are human imaginations. The long title poem, "The Auroras of Autumn," is a look backward at a life almost completed and forward toward an unknown future. Other poems in this book also examine the possibility of transcendence—that there might be something that goes on beyond this life, this earth. The poems examine philosophical and

Susanne Schuenke's 1982 painting *The Sea of Time* reflects the tension between reality and imagination, between the past and the present that underpins *The Auroras of Autumn.* The critic Lloyd Frankenberg said of the book's preoccupations, "Imagination and reality cannot exist, or be comprehended, except by means of each other. Yet Stevens must constantly be making the attempt to isolate them. . . . He writes constantly about the future. . . . He looks always for 'A new text of the world.'"

religious ideas without reaching any clear conclusions.

THE COLLECTED POEMS OF WALLACE STEVENS (1954).

Stevens's final assembly of his work, which appeared in the year before his death, shows the overall direction of his thought. Although the work is taken in succession from each of his individual volumes of poetry, the whole structure of thought is only visible in the collected poems. The poems begin with the spring of *Harmonium,* then pass through the summer and autumn of the following collections. The final section, "The Rock," was not published previously. Besides wintery poems, this section concludes with a new spring. The first line of the last poem is "At the earliest ending of winter," suggesting the coming of a new and unknown spring. Many poets have used the seasons as a metaphor for life, but Stevens revitalizes this old comparison. *The Collected Poems of Wallace Stevens* also allows the reader to trace how Stevens's focus and style evolved, from the early Florida poems to the last poems of farewell.

THE NECESSARY ANGEL: ESSAYS ON REALITY AND THE IMAGINATION (1951).

Paintings such as Salavador Dali's *Mountain Lake* (Tate Gallery, London) marked the radical departure with prevailing styles that characterized the art of the early decades of the twentieth century. This same desire for a new aesthetic, a new sound, fueled Stevens's poetry.

This volume collects essays on poetry that Stevens wrote throughout his career, many of which were given as public presentations on college campuses. The essays are useful for serious students of Stevens, because they discuss his ideas of poetry in prose form. They explain his ideas about how poetry expresses the various time periods in which it was created, resulting in different kinds of art. Stevens also expresses how each location has a character, which makes itself felt in its art.

OPUS POSTHUMOUS (1957; revised and reissued, 1989).

This collection, which appeared after Stevens's death, contains many poems that he chose not to include in *The Collected Poems of Wallace Stevens* as well as some of his essays and reviews. Most of the work in this volume is relatively easy to read; their lack of characteristic caution and indirectness may explain their exclusion from previous volumes. Nevertheless, these works are useful in presenting more clearly some of the ideas and positions Stevens explored throughout his life. The reviews are helpful as well; they indirectly describe, through his evaluation of others' work, what Stevens attempted to achieve in his own. His concern that poetry be grounded in the actual world is very apparent, for instance, in his favorable review of the poetry of Marianne Moore.

TRANSPORT TO SUMMER (1947).

This large collection includes Stevens's long philosophical poems on the nature of poetry. A long, complex work, it challenges the reader even with its titles, which include "Burghers of Petty Death," "Somnambulisma," and "Esthétique du Mal."

Perhaps only the dedicated Stevens scholar will appreciate this volume, but the collection's longest poem, "Notes Toward a Supreme Fiction," contains Stevens's most complete statement of what he was trying to achieve

Counterbalancing Stevens's novelty and experimentation was the anchor of heritage and his boyhood home. This 1851 print shows the Philadelphia and Reading railroad bridge where it crosses the Schuykill River.

through poetry. Stevens was attempting to define what he called a "Supreme Fiction," a human invention he thought would take the place of religion, which he believed no longer offered comfort and direction in life. This "fiction" he thought of, at least some of the time, as being the ultimate poetry. He had three requirements for his "supreme fiction," and he made these the topics of parts of the poem. These requirements were that the fiction must be abstract, must change, and must give pleasure. He wanted the supreme fiction to go beyond any particular art that was located in a time and place and limited to that time and place, and he wanted his fiction to be satisfying.

Resources

The Wallace Stevens Archive at the Huntington Library in San Marino, California contains most of Stevens's materials and includes nearly seven thousand items, including correspondence, manuscripts, awards, photos, and other mementos. The Houghton Library at Harvard University in Cambridge, Massachusetts, also has a collection of Stevens materials, including letters about translations of Stevens's work into Italian. Other sources of interest for students of Wallace Stevens include the following:

Wallace Stevens Journal. The Wallace Stevens Society sponsors the publication of *The Wallace Stevens Journal,* an invaluable resource of articles and poems, memoirs and bibliographies, and reviews of the latest Stevens scholarship. (http://www.clarkson.edu/wsj)

Alan Filreis's Home Page. Professor Alan Filreis of the University of Pennsylvania maintains a Web site with miscellaneous information about Stevens and good links to other Stevens sources, including a listserv for discussion of Stevens. (http://dept.english.upenn.edu/~afilreis/Stevens/home.html)

Audio Recordings. A cassette entitled *Wallace Stevens Reads* (1993), originally recorded in 1956, is available from Caedmon.

Video Recordings. Part eleven of the thirteen-part *Voices and Visions* poetry video series produced by the New York Center for Visual History and the Annenberg/CPB Project is devoted to the life and work of Wallace Stevens. It is entitled *Wallace Stevens: Man Made out of Words* (1988).

JANET MCCANN

William Styron

BORN: June 11, 1925, Newport News, Virginia
IDENTIFICATION: Late-twentieth-century southern writer and Pulitzer
Prize winner whose novels have addressed racism and the Holocaust.

William Styron's most popular and critically praised novels, *The Confessions of Nat Turner* (1967) and *Sophie's Choice* (1979) are connected, respectively, with racism and genocide. Although Styron engendered criticism suggesting that, as a white American Southerner, he had no right to take on the fictional voice of a black slave or of a Jew during the Holocaust, continuing critical assessment ensured his reputation as a major American writer. All Styron's works reflect, with powerful rhetoric and masterly structure, his willingness to face universal human problems without seeking an easy exit. He is continually concerned with physical pain, suffering, and human vulnerability, as well as with the importance of the past in affecting present behavior.

In 1990, after several years of psychological decline that included hospitalization for acute depression, Styron's career began a new chapter with the publication of a memoir entitled *Darkness Visible: A Memoir of Madness* (1990). Styron has also been, both in his journalistic writings and in interviews, an articulate opponent of the death penalty.

William Styron was born on June 11, 1925, in Newport News, Virginia, the only child of William Clark Styron and Pauline Margaret Abraham. W. C. Styron had come to Virginia from the small port town of Washington, North Carolina, and Pauline came from Uniontown, Pennsylvania. Styron would later describe his birthplace, the Tidewater region of Virginia, as "a very Southern part of the world."

Childhood. Styron's parents had married relatively late in life, and Pauline's pregnancy in the third year of the marriage, at age thirty-six, came as a surprise. Both of Styron's parents had strong artistic interests from an early age: Pauline as a drama student, singer, and music teacher and W. C. as an avid reader and writer. Financial pressures forced Styron's father to attend a technical school instead of a liberal arts college; W. C. studied engineering and went on to work for the rest of his life at a local shipyard.

Perhaps as a result of their own interests, when the young Styron showed an early aptitude for reading and language, his parents encouraged him. Throughout most of his childhood, Styron enjoyed a peaceful and relatively secure suburban existence. However, that world was overturned shortly after Styron turned fourteen, when his mother died of cancer after a long illness. His mother's death would have a life-long impact on Styron's personality and outlook.

Education. Styron was educated in the Newport News public school system and at Christchurch, an Episcopal boys' preparatory school in Middlesex County. Between 1942 and 1943 he attended Davidson College. That February, he enlisted in the U.S. Marine Corps before he became eligible for the draft and was assigned to officer candidate school (OCS) at Duke University in Durham, North Carolina. It was in the OCS that Styron's writing career began. He took a creative writing course at Duke from the novelist William Blackburn and published his first fiction—a Faulkneresque short story about a southern lynching—in a student anthology.

In 1944 Styron was ordered to boot camp at Parris Island, South

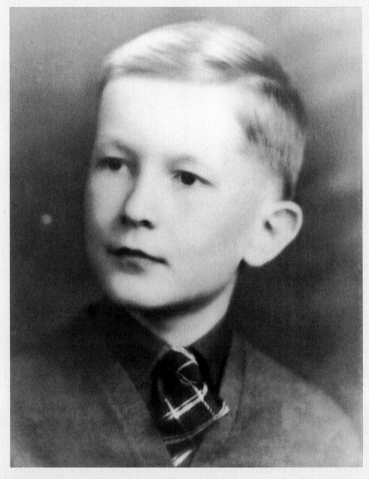

Styron as a little boy in Newport News, Virginia. From its beaches to its location on the borders of the South, his hometown would prove to shape his writing in subtle ways throughout his career.

U.S. Marine recruits practice handling their weapons at Parris Island, South Carolina, a few years before William Styron was to undergo the same training.

Carolina, eventually emerging as a second lieutenant. Styron's military unit was next in line for a planned assault on Japan's mainland, but in August 1945, it was spared from the confrontation by the atomic bombs dropped on Nagasaki and Hiroshima. After his military discharge, Styron completed his education at Duke, and in 1947 he landed a prestigious job as associate editor at McGraw-Hill publishers in New York City. However, he became disillusioned by the publishing world, which he found humorless and confining, and after six months he was fired.

The Fledgling Writer. For the next several years Styron drifted around New York, living on a small legacy from his grandmother and writing what would become his first novel, *Lie Down in Darkness*, which was published in 1951. The

book enjoyed moderate sales and received critical acclaim and honors, including the prestigious Prix de Rome. By this time Styron had moved to Paris, France, and had taken up with a group of young American expatriate writers, including George Plimpton, Peter Matthiessen, James Baldwin, James Jones, and Irwin Shaw. The group founded the *Paris Review*, which became one of the most influential literary journals of its generation.

While in Paris, Styron completed his second novel, *The Long March*, based on his military experience. It was published first serially in 1952 and later in book form by Knopf in 1956. Styron used the money from the Prix de Rome Fellowship for a sojourn in Italy, where he began what he described as his "big novel," published in 1960 as *Set This House on Fire*, a story of self-indulgent American intellectuals

Styron's first novel, *Lie Down in Darkness,* paved the way for the success to come. This publicity shot from 1952 accompanied the announcement that, as the second-ever recipient of the Prix de Rome prize, the young novelist would be taking up residence at the American Academy in Rome starting in October of that year.

Styron saw the material as a conjunction of themes close to his heart: the guilt and pain of Southerners over the issue of slavery and his personal and spiritual concerns and responsibilities of a fiction writer. The book that clarified Styron's technique for *The Confessions of Nat Turner,* he would later say, was Albert Camus's *L'Étranger* (1942; *The Stranger,* 1946), which consisted of a narrator reflecting back on his experiences from the perspective of a jail cell.

One of Styron's strongest supporters, both before and after the publication of the novel, was his friend the African American author James Baldwin, who lived with the Styrons while writing his novel *Another Country* (1962). Baldwin hailed *The Confessions of Nat Turner* as "less a 'historical novel' than a meditation on history" and suggested it might be the beginning of a "mutual history" of blacks and whites.

However, the critical accolades for *The Confessions of Nat Turner,* which included a Pulitzer Prize, were met in the politically volatile year of 1967 with vehement charges from a number of black scholars and activists that a white author had no right to interpret the black experience. That firestorm of criticism resulted the following year in a book of essays edited by John Henrik Clarke entitled *William Styron's "Nat Turner": Ten Black Writers Respond* (1968) as well as in death threats against Styron and his family.

Emotionally bruised but undaunted, Styron turned his attention to a new novel rooted in the psyche of a career military officer. He eventually shelved this work and began anew on a fictional reminiscence of his brief time in the New York publishing world. After innumerable twists and turns throughout five years of writing, this manuscript would become the story of a woman who survived the Nazi concentration camps and the death of a child but who could

in postwar Europe. The book received mixed reviews, which were better in Europe than in the United States and which were a generally chastening experience for Styron. During this time he also met and married Rose Burgunder, a Jewish poet from Maryland.

Styron returned to the United States with his new wife and settled in Roxbury, Connecticut. He began work on a book whose careful craftsmanship he resolved would redeem him from what he now considered the flawed work of *Set This House on Fire.* He spent the next several years meticulously researching and writing the novel that would become *The Confessions of Nat Turner,* based on a historical incident near Styron's birthplace, a failed 1831 slave rebellion whose instigator—the title character—was executed after supposedly dictating his own memoir from prison.

In this photograph from 1996, Styron and his wife, Rose, are in attendance at a reception honoring the visiting president of Ireland Mary Robinson.

which was published in 1990 with the title *Darkness Visible: A Memoir of Madness*—the title phrase taken from a description of Hell in John Milton's *Paradise Lost* (1667, 1674).

After the publication of *Darkness Visible*, which in part aimed to educate a general audience that depression is not a defect of character but rather a life-threatening physical disease, Styron became a popular speaker on the subject of clinical depression, to both general audiences and physicians' groups.

In 1993 Styron published *A Tidewater Morning: Three Tales from Youth*, a collection of what he described as "long short stories," on the topics of death and loss, war, and racism. He and his wife remained in Roxbury, Connecticut, with a second home in Vineyard Haven, Massachusetts.

not survive the emotional scars with which the experience left her. *Sophie's Choice*, published in 1979, received critical acclaim, best-seller status, and a lucrative sale of film rights. Meryl Streep, who portrayed the title character in the film version released in 1982, won an Academy Award for Best Actress in 1983 for her performance.

Ironically, at this time—the very peak of his career—Styron began to slide into a clinical depression, which became so acute that in 1985 he had to be hospitalized. After a slow recovery he returned to writing fiction and began a novel about his experience with the illness. However, he never felt satisfied with what he produced. Eventually his grapplings with madness and suicidal thoughts became the subject of a long essay for *Esquire* magazine. The outpouring of public response to the essay led Styron to develop it into a nonfiction book,

In addition to his accomplishments as a novelist, Styron is heralded for publicly acknowledging his clinical depression. His frank and open treatment of his condition came at a time when the illness was rarely discussed and still bore a societal stigma.

The scholar Melvin J. Friedman called William Styron "probably the least parochial and least regional of major contemporary Southern writers. His broad and far-ranging sympathies make him an author of international scope and consequence." Friedman's view is clearly reflected in the range of concerns that are raised in Styron's major novels.

Issues in Styron's Fiction. From the beginning of his career, Styron tackled a variety of weighty and controversial issues that are universal in theme. In his first novel, *Lie Down in*

Styron in 1967. As a writer, he was able to hang on the fringes of tradition, never fully committing to one style or school of influence.

Darkness, which recounts through flashback the life of a young Virginia woman who has committed suicide in New York City, critics pointed out a consistent theme of homages to William Faulkner—ranging from a funeral procession reminiscent of Faulkner's *As I Lay Dying* (1930) to a suicide victim's monologue that recalls *The Sound and the Fury* (1929). Although Styron outwardly seemed to be consciously declaring his heritage as a southern fiction writer, he later made this distinction in an interview with Robert K. Morris: "Basically, I guess, I am trying to make a distinction between Southern regionalism (which can be a very strong, fine thrust in literature), and my own work, which is Southern, but perhaps not regionally Southern."

The ever-protean relationship between reality and myth is another recurring theme in Styron's work. In addition to the often mythlike structure of *Lie Down in Darkness*, Styron's second novel, *Set This House on Fire*, treats the myth of Americans as, in Mark Twain's phrase, "innocents abroad" and also reflects on the topics of privilege, idleness, and ennui in a tone that at times resonates with attitudes expressed in F. Scott Fitzgerald's masterpiece, *The Great Gatsby* (1925).

In *The Confessions of Nat Turner*, biblical quotations—mainly violent and prophetic sections of the Old Testament—are a continuing echo and at times are contrasted in Turner's tug-of-war experience with the opposing values of New Testament teachings: love, forgiveness, and reconciliation.

The issues of slavery—evil, repression, and inhumanity—recur in the context of the Nazi Holocaust in the far more complex situations of *Sophie's Choice*, which many critics consider

Styron's most ambitious novel. In this book, Styron draws from and seamlessly unites a wide range of literary traditions: the urban Jewish novels of Saul Bellow and Philip Roth, the displaced southern narrator of Thomas Wolfe, and the wealth of Holocaust literature by Elie Wiesel and others.

The Styron scholar Melvin J. Friedman wrote that in *Sophie's Choice*, Styron transcends the regionalism of southern writers such as Eudora Welty and Flannery O'Connor. He aligns himself with the European modernists such as André Gide, André Malraux, and Thomas Mann, "especially with the way they secure everything in comfortably mythical terms."

The novel is one of many in which Styron uses violence as a window into contemporary society; in a later essay, he describes the Holocaust as "incomprehensible, and so awesomely central to our present-day conscious-

A group of mothers and their children arrive at the Auschwitz concentration camp in Poland in the early 1940s. Slavery and the Holocaust, Styron draws his inspiration from such large-scale social horrors, dissecting them and filtering them through the lives of his intricately drawn characters.

ness." The violence in Styron's novels ranges from social issues of war, genocide, and insurrection to the more personal: the suicides in *Sophie's Choice* and *Lie Down in Darkness* and the rape and murder of *Set This House on Fire*.

Another distinguishing characteristic of Styron's writing, both early and late, is his pas-

SOME INSPIRATIONS BEHIND STYRON'S WORK

William Styron's emotional affinity for the subjects of war and slavery—based both on his military experience and on his discovery that a distant ancestor owned slaves—is strong and surfaces repeatedly in his work. Graphic scenes of death, some of it accidental and unnecessary, abound in his early novel *The Long March*. Styron blurs the lines between the repression of slavery and the genocide of the Holocaust, casting both as offenses against humanity rather than mere racism or anti-Semitism.

HIGHLIGHTS IN STYRON'S LIFE

1925 William Styron is born on June 11 in Newport News, Virginia.

1939 Mother dies of cancer.

1942 Styron graduates from preparatory school and enrolls at Davidson College.

1944 Assigned to Marine Corps boot camp at Parris Island.

1945 Discharged from military after World War II peace treaty; attends Duke University.

1952 Wins Prix de Rome; moves to Europe.

1953 Marries Rose Burgunder in Rome, Italy.

1962 Publishes French translation of *Set This House on Fire* to critical acclaim.

1968 Awarded Pulitzer Prize for *The Confessions of Nat Turner*.

1980 Nominated for American Book Award and National Book Critics Circle Award for *Sophie's Choice*.

1985 Awarded Cino del Duca Prize in Paris; begins his descent into severe clinical depression

1990 Wins National Magazine Award for essay "Darkness Visible" in *Esquire*.

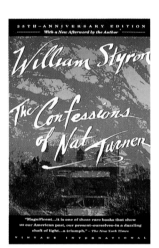

sion for grand and poetic language, including long meditations on American and European landscapes.

BIBLIOGRAPHY

Bryer, Jackson R., and Mary Beth Hatem. *William Styron: A Reference Guide*. Boston: G. K. Hall, 1978.

Casciato, Arthur D., and James L. W. West III, eds. *Critical Essays on William Styron*. Boston: G. K. Hall, 1982.

Cologne-Brookes, Gavin. *The Novels of William Styron: From Harmony to History*. Baton Rouge: Louisiana State University Press, 1995.

Crane, John Kenny. *The Root of All Evil: The Thematic Unity of William Styron's Fiction*. Columbia: University of South Carolina Press, 1984.

Flora, Joseph M., and Robert Bain, eds. *Fifty Southern Writers After 1900: A Bio-bibliographical Sourcebook*. New York: Greenwood Press, 1987.

Leon, Philip W., comp. *William Styron: An Annotated Bibliography of Criticism*. Westport, Conn.: Greenwood Press, 1978.

Morris, Robert K., and Irving Malin, eds. *The Achievement of William Styron*. Athens: University of Georgia Press, 1975.

Ross, Daniel W., ed. *The Critical Response to William Styron*. Westport, Conn.: Greenwood Press, 1995.

West, James L. W., III. *William Styron: A Descriptive Bibliography*. Boston: G. K. Hall, 1977.

———. *William Styron: A Life*. New York: Random House, 1998.

Reader's Guide to Major Works

THE CONFESSIONS OF NAT TURNER

Genre: Novel
Subgenre: Psychological realism
Published: New York, 1967
Time period: 1810–1831
Setting: Southeastern Virginia

Themes and Issues. In *The Confessions of Nat Turner*, William Styron uses the bare facts of an actual historic event to conjecture about the forces that turn the protagonist, by nature a meek and sensitive individual, into a religious fanatic driven to kill in order to lead his fellow slaves out of bondage. Those forces are the evils inherent in the two institutions that dominate the slave Nat Turner's life: slavery and Christianity.

The narrative sheds light on the monstrous societal blind spot that allowed people who considered themselves devout followers of Christ's message of love and brotherhood to simultaneously enslave, torture, and dehumanize fellow human beings on the basis of race. In one of the story's many ironies, Nat Turner's evolution into a man of action is set into motion by his learning to read from the books so cherished by his masters: the Bible and John Bunyan's *The Life and Death of Mr. Badman*

In Julia Eckel's 1934 painting *Revival* (Smithsoniam American Art Museum, Washington, D.C.), a preacher leads an impromptu service. Nat Turner, once defined by his role as a man of faith, is forced into a spiritual crisis by the hypocrises of a society that has enslaved him.

(1680). Turner's daily life within the system of slavery is shown to require a vast balancing act—outwardly pleasing his masters, while consciously playing roles to protect himself and to advance himself within the system.

The Plot. The novel opens after the main action of the story—a failed slave insurrection—has already ended, and its instigator is in jail awaiting execution. Nat Turner, who was a self-proclaimed preacher torn between the concepts of Christian love and Old Testament violence, finds himself unable to pray and feels that his God has abandoned him. Throughout the book, the story of Turner's life—and of his conversion from humble servant to murdering crusader—is told through flashbacks as he reflects on his past.

Turner's treatment as he passes through a series of owners ranges from savagery to relative kindness; one owner, Jeremiah Cobb, is so reasonable and supportive that even after Turner begins planning his rebellion, he resolves that Cobb will be one of the few white people "spared the sword." Ironically, in the end it becomes Cobb who officially hands down Turner's sentence of death by hanging.

Another white person who befriends Turner along the way is Margaret Whitehead, the shy wallflower daughter of one of his owners, who asks him to comment on her poetry and tells him that he is the only person in her life in whom she can confide. Margaret discusses Scripture with Turner, including the verse "perfect love casteth out fear," and expresses to him her puzzlement over why African Americans permit themselves to remain enslaved.

Turner teaches himself to read by sneaking books from the library of an early owner, Samuel Turner. When the owner finds out that Turner can read, he does not punish him but instead rewards him: apprenticing him to learn carpentry and promising to emancipate him when he turns twenty-five. Samuel is unable to keep the promise because the plantation's failing fortunes force him to sell it, and Turner's new owner, a minister named Alexander Eppes, proves to be the cruelest of all. After trying unsuccessfully to rape Turner, Eppes assigns him to hard labor and eventually sells him to Thomas Moore. When Moore discovers Turner's reading ability, he beats him for it.

For the next ten years, Nat leads a double life—outwardly obedient to Moore's commands but secretly studying his Bible, preaching to his fellow slaves about personal dignity and the inevitability of rebellion, and gradually recruiting a small army with an ambitious goal. Convinced that he has a mandate from God, Turner plans for the group to destroy the town's plantations and farms, to kill the whites, to attack the neighboring village of Jerusalem and seize its armory, and then to establish their guerrilla headquarters in a remote swamp.

However, when the time for the rebellion finally comes, in 1831, everything immediately begins to go wrong. The group attacks its first farmhouse, and Turner bungles the killing of the farmer. Another slave, named Will, has to take over, killing the man and his wife and then berating Turner in front of the group for being a poor leader. Turner, in a panic, decides that the only way he can regain control is to show his seriousness by killing Margaret Whitehead, which he does. The killing so disturbs him that he allows another white girl to escape, and she sounds the alarm that leads to the rebels' capture before they can do any more killing.

In jail Turner is provided a lawyer, Thomas Gray, but because the lawyer concurs with the sentencing, the gesture is only a symbolic one. Still, Gray is intrigued by Turner and visits his cell for a series of conversations. In one such conversation, Gray decries Christianity for causing only "misery and suffering for untold generations," and in another he taunts Turner by arguing that the insurrection failed because the majority of the slaves had remained faithful and defended their masters. On the morning of the execution Gray gives Turner a Bible, but Turner does not open it. Turner goes to the gallows thinking back on his friendship with Margaret and their conversations about Christian love.

William H. Johnson's *Nat Turner* graphically captures the final chapter in the slave's life. A tragic and complex figure, Turner was a man whose righteous indignation resolves itself in a rash act of violence.

Analysis. One of Styron's most impressive achievements in *The Confessions of Nat Turner* is his portrayal of Turner as a complex, believable, and conflicted character rather than as the one-dimensional warrior hero of abolitionist folklore. It was exactly this achievement that drew an outpouring of protest from many readers in the African American community, who charged that Styron's vision of Nat Turner was itself racist and a distortion of the historical record. Styron's portrayal of Turner's friendship with Margaret, in particular, and his supposed sexual fascination with white women was a main target of the critics' attacks. Styron's defenders pointed out that the character of Turner is depicted as a natural product of a system that had no place for a black individual with sensitivity or intellectual curiosity. A generation after the controversy, though, the book's status as a classic of American literature seemed ensured.

SOURCES FOR FURTHER STUDY

Betts, Richard A. "*The Confessions of Nat Turner* and the Uses of Tragedy." *College Language Association Journal* 27, no. 4 (June 1984): 419–435.

Casciato, Arthur D., and James L. W. West III. "William Styron and the Southampton Insurrection." *American Literature: A Journal of Literary History, Criticism, and Bibliography* 52, no. 4 (1981): 564–577.

Clarke, John Henrik, ed. *William Styron's Nat Turner: Ten Black Writers Respond.* Boston: Beacon Press, 1968.

Mallard, James M. "The Unquiet Dust: The Problem of History in Styron's *The Confessions of Nat Turner*." *Mississippi Quarterly: The Journal of Southern Culture* 36, no. 4 (1983): 525–543.

SOPHIE'S CHOICE
Genre: Novel
Subgenre: Psychological realism
Published: New York, 1979
Time period: Summer 1947
Setting: Brooklyn, New York

Themes and Issues. Inhumanity, the burden of history, the boundaries of individual and collective guilt, the meaning of ethics in an impossible situation—all are themes woven with great subtlety and emotional impact through Styron's haunting and thought-provoking novel *Sophie's Choice*. The title character's life was forever scarred by her experience in the Nazi concentration camp at Auschwitz during the Holocaust and by the guilt she bears for her actions and choices against a background of unimaginable atrocities. The story's young narrator, who befriends and later falls in love with Sophie, has his own share of guilt, not only for the part his ancestors played in maintaining slavery but also for his inability to rescue Sophie from her past.

The Plot. A twenty-two-year-old man, a Virginia native who still goes by his prep-school nickname of Stingo, is living in

---

LONG FICTION

1951 Lie Down in Darkness
1956 The Long March (serial, 1952)
1960 Set This House on Fire
1967 The Confessions of Nat Turner
1979 Sophie's Choice

PLAY

1972 In the Clap Shack

SHORT FICTION

1993 A Tidewater Morning: Three Tales from Youth

NONFICTION

1982 This Quiet Dust
1990 Darkness Visible: A Memoir of Madness

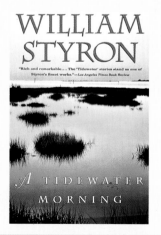

WILLIAM STYRON

"Rich and remarkable.... The 'Tidewater' stories stand as one of Styron's finest works."—*Los Angeles Times Book Review*

A TIDEWATER MORNING

Brooklyn on a small inheritance and writing a novel, after being fired from a prestigious Manhattan publishing job. He becomes increasingly curious about his upstairs neighbors, whose wild, overheard behavior ranges from passionate lovemaking to brutal quarrels. One evening Stingo inadvertently stumbles into one of the couple's fights and is greeted with a torrent of insults from Sophie's partner, Nathan, who then storms off and leaves them both alone.

The next morning, Sophie and Nathan—now all smiles and charm—knock on Stingo's door and invite him to spend the day with them at Coney Island. Stingo warily accepts, mainly in order to see more of Sophie. Surprisingly, the trio quickly become fast friends. However, the more Stingo learns of Sophie and Nathan, the more troubled he becomes. He glimpses a row of numbers tattooed on Sophie's wrist, his first hint of her tragic past. He learns that she is a native of Poland who spent twenty months in an Auschwitz concentration camp, during which she was separated from her children, whom she never saw again. Nathan apparently met Sophie in New York—malnourished, severely depressed, and with lingering illnesses from her inhumane treatment—and took her under his wing, getting her medical treatment and false teeth and moving into the apartment next door to her.

Stingo is frightened and dumbfounded by Nathan's occasional habit of seemingly pointless violent rages and by Nathan's emotional abuse and cruelty toward both Stingo and Sophie. After one cataclysmic fight, during which Nathan accuses Sophie of anti-Semitism and unfaithfulness and viciously ridicules Stingo's novel, Nathan and Sophie break up and decide to move out of the building. Stingo convinces Sophie to stay at least through the weekend, and in the process she tells him even darker secrets about Nathan and their relationship: that he is addicted to drugs and has tried to persuade her to commit suicide with him.

Sophie also reveals that her own front is a false one as well. Not Jewish herself, she tried, while at Auschwitz, to seduce the camp commandant in order to gain her children's freedom. She also tried to use to her advantage the fact that her father was a violent anti-Semite who called for exterminating the Jews—revelations that show Nathan's outbursts in a new light. She also refused, out of fear for her children, to join the Polish resistance and saw many of her friends in the movement killed.

Nathan soon returns, begging Sophie's forgiveness, and she eagerly takes him in. Then Stingo encounters Nathan's brother, who reveals even more dark truths: Nathan is not the wealthy scientific researcher he claims to be but rather a paranoid schizophrenic on trial leave from a mental hospital, a fact that not even Sophie knows. Before long, Nathan returns to his old manic ways—this time accusing Sophie of sleeping with Stingo and threatening to come back to the apartment building and kill them both.

Stingo persuades Sophie to go to Virginia with him, where he plans to marry her and settle down. On the train ride, he discovers that her misery is apparently bottomless, when she confesses the "choice" of the book's title. On her arrival at Auschwitz, a sadistic doctor working for the gestapo forced her to choose which of her two children would go immediately to the gas chamber and which would be spared to go to the children's camp. Under duress and in horror, Sophie chooses her daughter for the gas chamber and now has imprinted on her memory forever the scene of the girl being led away in fright and confusion, hugging her beloved flute.

The next morning, Stingo wakes to find that Sophie has returned to Brooklyn. He decides to travel on to Virginia alone but soon realizes that he cannot abandon Nathan and Sophie. He goes to Brooklyn but discovers that his two friends, in a suicide pact, have died in each other's arms.

Analysis. In *Sophie's Choice* Styron creates a masterpiece of dramatic structure and suspense, and his portrayal of Sophie's intensely individual web of guilt over the events of her past is one of the most complex and compelling characterizations in twentieth-century fiction. Although Nathan's inner life is never explored on a similar level of detail, his personality and family background clearly make him a volatile foil for Sophie, lending credibility to the idea that his mental illness would crescendo into obsessions with the Holocaust and with Nazi war criminals. Stingo, torn between wanting to rescue his friends and knowing he cannot, also has to live with his own share of guilt over what he could have done differently. His main failing, as he realizes when he collapses emotionally during the funeral, is that "I was unprepared to weep for all humanity."

SOURCES FOR FURTHER STUDY

Cologne-Brookes, Gavin. *The Novels of William Styron: From Harmony to History*. Baton Rouge: Louisiana State University Press, 1995.

Ross, Daniel W., ed. *The Critical Response to William Styron*. Westport, Conn.: Greenwood Press, 1995.

Sirlin, Rhoda. *William Styron's "Sophie's Choice": Crime and Self-Punishment*. Ann Arbor, Mich.: UMI Research Press, 1990.

Bathers soak up the sun in Thomas Hart Benton's 1922 painting *Self-Portrait with Rita* (National Portrait Gallery, Washington, D.C.). The fun and frivolity of a day at the beach is a mask for the dark conflicts lacing Nathan and Sophie's relationship.

Other Works

LIE DOWN IN DARKNESS (1951). The title of William Styron's first novel is taken from the seventeenth-century British philosopher Sir Thomas Browne's treatise on mortality, *Hydriotaphia, Urne-Buriall* (1658), in which Browne says, "It cannot be long before we lie down in darkness and have our light in ashes." Styron's novel begins with the suicide of a young Virginia woman named Peyton Loftis, who leaped from a building in New York City. Because officials have difficulty ascertaining her identity, her body narrowly misses being buried in Potter's Field.

Her body is carried home by train to Port Warwick, Virginia, for the funeral, and only two cars follow the hearse in the procession. In one is Peyton's mother and her minister; in the other is Peyton's father and his mistress. During a number of complicating incidents, including car trouble, the four characters remember both Peyton's past and their own. In the final section of the book, Peyton herself gives a soliloquy in which she reflects on her past and her reasons for committing suicide.

Peyton's mother, Helen, is emotionally unsettled and recalls giving all of her time and love to Peyton's older sister, Maudie, who was crippled and retarded from birth. Peyton's father, Milton, an alcoholic who married Helen during wartime, made the physically "perfect" Peyton the target of his damagingly obsessive love.

In Anna Belle Lee's 1924 painting *Baptism,* figures clad in white publicly avow their faith. A baptism scene such as this, marking a spiritual cleansing, lends Styron's *Lie Down in Darkness* a tenuous, albeit powerful, ending.

Helen recalls blaming both her husband and Peyton for Maudie's untimely death. After shutting them both out of her life, she turned to religion, to her minister, and ultimately, to mental illness. Milton retreated to alcohol and to a mistress, Dolly Bonner. Peyton follows in her father's footsteps of drinking and promiscuity. At her wedding to Harry, a Jewish artist from New York, a drunken Milton makes sexual advances to his daughter.

Peyton moves with Harry to New York, leaves him when she discovers his affairs with other men, and finally takes her own life. After the funeral Helen and Milton have a violent argument in which he tries to choke her, and they separately leave the cemetery.

A hallmark of the book is Styron's skillful handling of scene shifts and multiple points of view. Unconventionally, the novel ends with a revival meeting and baptismal service at a black church, which ends—as the book began—with the sound of a distant train: "Another blast from the whistle, a roar, a gigantic sound; and it seemed to soar into the dusk beyond and above them forever, with a noise, perhaps, like the clatter of the opening of everlasting gates and doors—passed swiftly on—toward Richmond, the North, the oncoming night."

THIS QUIET DUST (1982). Unlike many compilations of successful authors' essays and journalism, Styron's collection—despite its range of subjects from the history of slavery to the turbulent 1968 Democratic National Convention in Chicago—exhibits a thematic unity and insight into the author's mind that makes it an especially valuable companion piece for readers studying his major novels.

In the title essay, Styron recounts his discovery of the historical figure Nat Turner, largely a footnote in history before the author's years of research and writing produced the award-winning and controversial *The Confessions of Nat Turner*.

In "The Service," Styron reflects on both the madness and the inevitability of war, offering perspective on famous and infamous warriors ranging from General Douglas MacArthur to Lieutenant William Calley, who was tried for the 1968 My Lai massacre of civilians in Vietnam.

Two of the most high-profile essays of the collection are "The Death-in-Life of Benjamin Reid," and "Benjamin Reid: Aftermath," which detail Styron's involvement with Reid, a convict who had been on death row for four years when the author interviewed him for an *Esquire* profile. Styron did not dispute Reid's guilt, but the essay about the sad circumstances of the prisoner's early life so moved the public that prominent attorneys and professors succeeded in getting Reid's sentence commuted to life with possible parole. Reid earned his high school diploma and at a parole hearing was offered a college scholarship. Styron was to offer Reid a room in his home until permanent plans could be made for his housing. Shortly before his release, Reid escaped, stole a car, kidnapped a woman and her children, and raped the woman before being captured. Styron's essays offer no easy answers to a grim question that mocks prisons as well as the people who would reform them.

In "Chicago: 1968" Styron recounts his experiences as a delegate for presidential candidate Senator Eugene McCarthy at the Democratic National Convention, complete with sit-ins, folksingers, and the Chicago mayor Richard Daley's call for the use of special police patrols and tear gas to quell the unrest.

Resources

The W. R. Perkins Library at Duke University is the major repository of William Styron's papers, including a holograph of *Sophie's Choice* and many other typescripts, manuscripts, proofs, and personal letters. Other sources of interest for students of William Styron include the following:

Video Recording. *William Styron: The Way of the Writer* features interviews with the author's family, professors, and other authors. It first aired on PBS in 1997 and is a coproduction of The New York Center for Visual History, Thirteen/WNET, and Little Bear/France 3. (http://www.pbs.org/wnet/ammasters/template.html)

Interview. Styron was interviewed in 1998 by one of his biographers. The conversation, which also features Styron's daughter Susanna, may be listened to on line at "Cyber LC," a cybercast from the Library of Congress. (http://www.broadcast.com/news/events/loc/styron/locsite/)

William Styron Web Site. This is a useful source of information about Styron's writing and speaking engagements. The site also contains a collection of family photographs, quotes, articles, interviews, and book reviews. (http://www.sirius.com/~fillius/styron.htm)

CARROLL DALE SHORT

Amy Tan

BORN: February 19, 1952, Oakland, California
IDENTIFICATION: Late twentieth-century Asian American fiction writer known for her explorations of Chinese American women's issues.

Amy Tan's best-known work, *The Joy Luck Club* (1989), added to the wave of literary creativity and reader interest about Asian American subjects that had been inaugurated in the 1970s by writers such as the playwright Frank Chin and the novelist Maxine Hong Kingston. Partially based on her own family's experiences, Tan's novels explore the relationships and heartaches of Asian immigrant mothers and their native-born American daughters, appealing to feminist readers and those interested in intergenerational and multicultural issues. Although her other novels have not been as widely acclaimed as her first, Tan's works are taken seriously by critics and scholars and are frequently assigned in schools and colleges.

The Writer's Life

Amy Tan was born on February 19, 1952, in Oakland, California. She was given the Chinese name An-mei, *Mei* meaning "America" or "beautiful," and *An* meaning "peace" or "blessing." Her parents, John Tan and Daisy Chan, each had emigrated from China. They had two other children, boys born in 1950 and 1954.

John Tan had been an electrical engineer in China but became a Baptist minister in the United States; he had also worked for the United States Information Service during World War II. Daisy Tan came from a wealthy Shanghai family, but when Daisy was nine, her mother was widowed, was tricked into concubinage, and then committed suicide. When Daisy reached adulthood, she entered into an arranged marriage; before this marriage ended in divorce, she had a son, who died early, and three daughters whom she had to leave in China when she emigrated.

Childhood. Tan grew up in several California towns: Fresno, Oakland, San Francisco, and Santa Clara. Like many immigrant children in the United States, Tan harbored questions and doubts about her racial and cultural identity. For instance, she remembers putting a clothespin on her nose and dreaming about plastic surgery to Westernize her features. Furthermore, her parents spoke Chinese at home, whereas her teachers spoke English at school. Tan found her English classes more difficult than her mathematics classes. When she was fifteen, both her father and her elder brother died suddenly of brain tumors.

Daisy Tan decided upon a change of scene and took her surviving children to Europe. The

Tan drew on her own experiences growing up, writing her breakthrough novel *The Joy Luck Club.* Here, a scene from the film version probably closely replicates a scene from the author's own life, a trip to the bakery with her mother.

family settled in Montreux, Switzerland, where Tan attended an English-language school. As a teenager, she rebelled against her mother, dating a German with drug connections. Daisy hired a private detective to engineer a drug raid, and a chastened Tan realized that she had been dating a criminal and an escaped mental patient. At age seventeen, she graduated from the Institut Monte Rosa Internationale, Montreux.

The Future Writer. Tan had won an essay contest at the age of eight with an entry entitled "What the Library Means to Me"; after this experience she dreamed of becoming a writer. However, her parents felt that writing was insufficiently lucrative and preferred that their daughter become a neurosurgeon and concert pianist.

The strong Chinese American presence in San Francisco helped shape Tan's meditations on women who had immigrated and those who were born here.

After Tan's high school graduation, the family moved back to the San Francisco area. In 1969 Tan enrolled in Linfield College, in McMinnville, Oregon. After a year, however, she transferred, against her mother's wishes, to San Jose City College and then to San Jose State University. She obtained both a bachelor's degree in linguistics and English and a master's degree in linguistics from San Jose State University. She began doctoral studies at the University of California in Santa Cruz and Berkeley but decided instead to work with mentally retarded citizens and later with handicapped children.

Writing for Business and Pleasure. Tan soon turned to freelance technical and business writing, completing manuals for corporations such as AT&T and IBM, and becoming so successful that she was able to purchase a home for her mother. However, success turned her into a workaholic, and she sometimes worked as many as ninety hours in a week. She sought therapy to combat her tendency to overwork, but when her therapist regularly fell asleep on her, she decided to try writing instead.

To prepare herself to write fiction, Tan began to read widely in the work of contemporary female authors and was especially drawn to Louise Erdrich's *Love Medicine* (1984). She then wrote her first short story, "Endgame," about a girl chess champion's conflicts with her mother. In 1985 that story gained her entry into the Squaw Valley Community, a fiction writers' workshop run by the novelist Oakley Hall. There Tan came under the tutelage of short-story writer Molly Giles, who helped her revise "Endgame" for publication in *FM Magazine* and later in *Seventeen*. The story also appears in *The Joy Luck Club* as "Rules of the Game."

Giles sent "Endgame" to the California-based literary agent Sandra Dijkstra, who encouraged Tan to send more material. In July 1987, Tan submitted synopses of related stories as an idea for a book. Dijkstra liked Tan's concept and began marketing it under its working title, "Wind and Water," a literal translation of *feng shui*, the Chinese art of geomancy, or determining one's fortune through geography and the elements.

Tan's mother had suffered an apparent heart attack in 1986, and Tan resolved to be more attentive to her mother and her tales. In October, 1987, she accompanied her mother to China, Tan's first visit to her ancestral homeland. After returning to California, Tan discovered that her agent had negotiated a fifty-thousand-dollar book advance with G. P. Putnam's Sons. Tan quit freelance writing, devoted herself to fiction, and in four months completed the manuscript published as *The Joy Luck Club*.

Success Story. Released in 1989, *The Joy Luck Club* received national acclaim from reviewers in the *Los Angeles Times* and the *New York Times*, on whose best-seller list it remained for almost a year. It was short-listed for the National Book Award, nominated for the National Book Critics Circle Award, and received the Bay Area Book Reviewers Award for fiction along with the Commonwealth Club Gold Award. Vintage bought the paperback rights for just over one million dollars. The book was translated into at least twenty languages, including Chinese. *The Joy Luck Club* was released as a film in 1993 and became a box-office success. Its screenplay was cowritten by Amy Tan and Ronald Bass, and the film was directed by the well-respected Asian American filmmaker Wayne Wang.

Tan's second novel, *The Kitchen God's Wife* (1991), was also a widely lauded best-seller, and its paperback rights fetched a higher price than those of its predecessor. A third novel, *The Hundred Secret Senses* (1995), continued Tan's commercial and popular success, although its reviews were more mixed than those of her first novel. In addition to these works, Tan has published several essays and two children's books— *The Moon Lady* (1992) and *The Chinese Siamese Cat* (1994).

Tan settled in San Francisco with her husband, Louis DeMattei, a tax attorney. She maintained her membership in Molly Giles's writing group, meeting regularly in Tan's Presidio Heights home.

Tan was not long enticed by the vibrant urban life of Berkeley, California, as seen here at the University of California at Berkeley in 1972. She soon turned her attention elsewhere, abandoning her doctoral studies to work with handicapped children.

HIGHLIGHTS IN TAN'S LIFE

1952   Amy Tan is born on February 19 in Oakland, California.

1952–1966 Lives with family in several San Francisco Bay Area towns.

1967   Both her father and elder brother die suddenly of brain tumors.

1968   Tan moves with mother and surviving brother to Montreux, Switzerland; attends English-language school until graduation.

1969   Graduates from Institut Monte Rosa Internationale in Montreux; returns to United States with family; enrolls in Linfield College, McMinnville, Oregon.

1970   Transfers to San Jose City College, California.

1971   Transfers to San Jose State University, from which she earns both a bachelor's and a master's degree.

1976   Begins doctoral studies at the University of California in Santa Cruz and Berkeley but abandons studies.

1976   Begins employment as social worker and later as a freelance business and technical writer in the Bay Area.

1985   Decides to write fiction; joins Squaw Valley Community; studies with author Molly Giles.

1987   Travels to China with mother.

1989   Publishes *The Joy Luck Club*.

1991   Publishes *The Kitchen God's Wife*.

1992   Publishes *The Moon Lady*, a children's book.

1993   Film version of *The Joy Luck Club* is released.

1994   Publishes *The Chinese Siamese Cat*, a children's book.

1995   Publishes *The Hundred Secret Senses*.

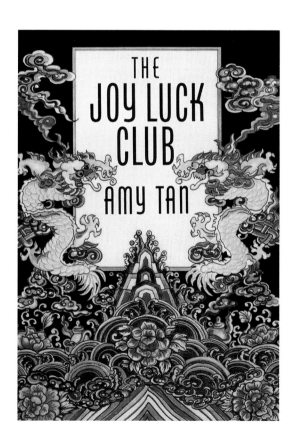

The Writer's Work

Amy Tan has written long and short fiction, children's books, and essays and has collaborated on a screenplay. She is, however, best known for her work in long fiction, particularly in the genres of the novel and the short-story cycle, or the composite novel. Tan's long fiction is notable for its deeply moving portrayals of women, especially Chinese American women, both immigrant and American-born. Tan explores in depth the psychology of feminine relationships, between mothers and daughters and among siblings and peers. She characteristically employs complex narrative patterns and intricate structures in her work. Her narratives also capture the tone of Chinese "talk-story," part of the oral Chinese folk storytelling tradition. Her characters speak authentically and expressively in a distinctive and supple language that blends Chinese phraseology and syntax with American idiom. Furthermore, the action of her works is often enriched by allusions to Chinese myth, folklore, and history.

Issues in Tan's Fiction.

Broadly speaking, Tan's fiction takes as its central issues women's lives and concerns. Her work focuses more specifically on the lives and concerns of Chinese American women, of both the American-born and the immigrant generations. This focus reflects Tan's personal experiences as a Chinese American woman born in America of immigrant parents. Much of Tan's work concerns the individuation, or the finding of one's self-identity, and the empowerment of women in varying social and familial contexts, whether in a child's shaping of self, an immigrant's search for a place in a new society, or a wife's struggle against an oppressive relationship.

Tan recounts in detail the courage, endurance, and astuteness of women in a patriarchal Chinese society. At the same time she describes the struggles and successes of immigrants who must become assimilated into a country where the language, customs, and

Donning a wig, Tan fronts for the Rock Bottom Remainders, a group formed entirely of writers, in May 1998. Beside her, playing the guitar, is horror novelist Stephen King.

prejudices offer great difficulties and exhilarating discoveries. She depicts through vivid situations and empathetic characters both the horrors of war in China and the dysfunction of families in the contemporary United States.

People in Tan's Fiction.
Tan's major characters are women of Chinese descent. Her most memorable women are characters in or from China, ranging from the near-aristocratic to the peasant class. Her American-born women characters, such as Waverley Jong and Jing-Mei (June) Woo in *The Joy Luck Club* and Olivia in *A Hundred Secret Senses*, have neither the tragic pathos nor the spiritual depth of their Chinese-born counterparts Lindo Jong, Suyuan Woo, or Kwan. *The Kitchen God's Wife* is dominated by Weili, whose life in China is full of drama and pathos.

Tan's Chinese-born women must survive wars, surmount societal conditions approximating slavery, and endure familial or marital abuse. They overcome these conditions through their resilience, their intelligence, their toughness of character, and their reserves of psychological and spiritual strength stemming from special abilities or gifts derived from Chinese beliefs. Thus, Lindo Jong of *The Joy Luck Club* gains power through her ability to read the geomantic forces governing a situation. Similarly, in *The Hundred Secret Senses*, Kwan's *yin* eyes that enable her to see and communicate with the dead are a medium's gift that Tan may have derived from the female principle of the Taoist yin-yang or from Kwan Yin, the Chinese goddess of mercy.

Women's Individuation and Empowerment.
The dominant theme of Tan's work is that of women's achieving self-identity and empowerment through their various relationships:

Zifen Qian's 1993 painting *A Sunny Day with Gentle Breeze* recalls the daughters that populate much of Tan's fiction. They are strong, independent figures, trying to step out of the long shadows cast by their mothers.

mother to daughter, woman to lover, and woman to another woman, such as a sibling, friend, or rival. The mother-daughter relationship is the one most intensely and movingly expressed in Tan's work, which suggests that the most satisfying kind of individuation for women involves unification rather than a separation with the mother.

Thus Jing-Mei Woo of *The Joy Luck Club* and Pearl in *The Kitchen God's Wife* must work out their troubled relationships with their mothers before they can feel secure and sure about themselves. Jing-Mei's taking her mother's place in the mission to locate her lost sisters in China brings her to an understanding of her mother's hopes and love for her and a feeling of completeness. In *The Kitchen God's Wife*, Tan emphasizes the importance of communication between mother and daughter: Weili's effort to

In *The Hundred Secret Senses*, Kwan is graced with *yin* eyes, which allow her to access the events of the distant past. Naoki Okamoto's 1990 untitled painting suggests this gift, the eye that sees all, that is everywhere.

tell fully and candidly her life story to her daughter Pearl exorcises the ghosts of her past. Weili's sharing gives Pearl courage to tell her mother her own secret. This establishment of communication between mother and daughter heals the elder and completes the younger.

BIBLIOGRAPHY

Huntley, E. D. *Amy Tan: A Critical Companion.* Westport, Conn.: Greenwood Press, 1998.

Kramer, Barbara. *Amy Tan: Author of "The Joy Luck Club."* Springfield, N.J.: Enslow, 1996.

Ling, Amy. *Between Worlds: Women Writers of Chinese Ancestry.* New York: Pergamon Press, 1990.

Pearlman, Mickey, and Katharine Usher Henderson. *Inter/View: Talks with America's Writing Women.* Lexington: University Press of Kentucky, 1990.

Smorada, Claudia Kovach. "Side-Stepping Death: Ethnic Identity, Contradiction, and the Mother(land) in Amy Tan's Novels." *Fu Jen Studies: Literature and Linguistics* 24 (1991): 31–45.

Wong, Sau-ling. "'Sugar Sisterhood': Situating the Amy Tan Phenomenon." In *The Ethnic Canon*, edited by David Palumbo-Liu. Minneapolis: University of Minnesota Press, 1995.

SOME INSPIRATIONS BEHIND TAN'S WORK

The source of many of Amy Tan's most memorable female characters appears to be her mother, Daisy Tan, and her "talk stories" about life in China. In *The Joy Luck Club*, for instance, several of Suyuan's experiences in China, such as her abandonment of her babies during World War II, are derived from Daisy Tan's own experience. The tribulations of An-Mei Hsu's mother, such as forced concubinage and suicide, appear to be based on those of Daisy Tan's mother. Daisy Tan's experiences of an unhappy childhood, abusive first marriage, divorce, and happy remarriage seem also to provide the subject matter that Tan used in creating the character of Weili in *The Kitchen God's Wife*.

Tan was inspired in her literary craft by the examples of several female writers. Maxine Hong Kingston had successfully pioneered a feminist approach to the Chinese American experience and used the talk-story as a narrative device. In preparation for her serious attempts at fiction writing, Tan had also read extensively in the works of such twentieth-century women writers as Alice Munro, Eudora Welty, Flannery O'Connor, Amy Hemphill, and, above all, Louise Erdrich. Erdrich's short-story cycle *Love Medicine*, which employed multiple Native American narrators spanning several generations, was an especially powerful inspiration for *The Joy Luck Club*, likewise a short-story cycle employing many narrators from two generations of Chinese Americans.

Reader's Guide to Major Works

THE JOY LUCK CLUB

Genre: Novel

Subgenre: Short-story cycle/composite novel

Published: New York, 1989

Time period: From 1900 to 1970s

Setting: China; California

Themes and Issues. Two themes figure prominently in *The Joy Luck Club*: mother-daughter (mis)communication and women's individuation, or developing self-identity, and empowerment. These themes are developed through a drama of loss and recovery against a Chinese or Chinese American backdrop.

Communication difficulties are readily apparent in the book's narrative structure. Four mother-daughter pairs of first-person narrators provide multiple points of view with many instances of misunderstanding. Linguistic miscommunications occur frequently also, although Amy Tan successfully concocts a patois, or blended dialect, for her immigrant Chinese mothers to speak with authenticity, humor, and irony. For instance, when Waverley tells her mother, "I'm my own person," her mother thinks to herself: "How can she be her own person? When did I give her up?"

One example of individuation and empowerment is illustrated in the chapter entitled

Forced to abandon her young daughters during the Japanese occupation of China, Suyuan, played by Kieu Chinh in the film version of *The Joy Luck Club*, eventually immigrates to San Francisco where she is haunted by her past deed.

"The Red Candle," when Lindo Jong suffers a demeaning marriage in China to an impotent husband whose family blames her for the couple's childlessness. Lindo empowers herself by playing on her mother-in-law's superstitions in order to annul her marriage, and she also makes a match between her hapless husband and a maid pregnant with an illegitimate child.

In this chapter, the symbol of power is the wind, which Lindo observes extinguishing the red candle's symbolic marital flame. Lindo adopts the image to describe her self-empowerment: "I was strong . . . like the wind." Wind is a traditional metaphor for power in both Judeo-Christian and Chinese traditions. In the Bible, the Holy Ghost is represented as a rushing wind, and in *feng shui*, the Chinese art of geomancy, the word "*feng*" itself means "wind."

The Plot. The book opens with loss and ends with recovery. Its initial setting is the Chinese American community in San Francisco in the 1970s. The Joy Luck Club is a group of four immigrant Chinese women who gather regularly to play mahjong, a game similar to hearts or bridge played with domino-like tiles instead of cards. The club has lost a member, Suyuan, who has recently died, and her daughter Jingmei, called June by her American friends, has been asked to replace her.

The narrative reveals that during World War II, Suyuan suffered a terrible loss: She was forced to abandon her two daughters from her first marriage in China. Suyuan had always believed that the girls were dead, but her friends have discovered that they are alive. The women want June to go to China to seek out the children and unite with them as her mother would have done if she were alive. The women insist they would want their own daughters to continue something important that they had left unfinished.

June reluctantly accepts the women's request. Eventually, in a culminating moment of recovery, she is happily and tearfully united with her half-sisters. In the process she comes to an understanding of her mother's hopes, sorrows, and dreams. June's foray into her memories is paralleled by those of the other club women, who, with their daughters, share their memories of their lives in China with their mothers and of their lives in America with their own daughters.

Analysis. Structurally, *The Joy Luck Club*, like Geoffrey Chaucer's *The Canterbury Tales* (1387–1400) or its immediate model, Louise Erdrich's *Love Medicine*, is a compilation of linked first-person narratives. Just as Chaucer employs the narrative frame of a pilgrimage, suggesting the journey of life, so Tan uses the mahjong game, suggesting the game of life. A fitting metaphor for a narrative filled with voyages and culture clashes, the game of mahjong is played by four persons seated figuratively at

---

LONG FICTION

1989 The Joy Luck Club
1991 The Kitchen God's Wife
1995 The Hundred Secret
      Senses

CHILDREN'S LITERATURE

1992 The Moon Lady
1994 The Chinese Siamese Cat

NONFICTION

1990 "The Language of
      Discretion" (in The State
      of the Language, ed.
      Christopher Ricks and
      Leonard Michaels)

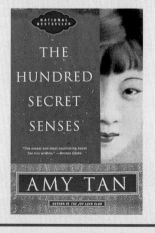

the four corners of the world. Indeed, spatial metaphors recur throughout the book and are related to the Chinese art of geomancy, *feng shui*, which means literally "wind and water," the book's original draft title.

In keeping with this mahjong-like spatialization, the contents of the book are also symmetrically fourfold: There are four parts, each containing four episodes. The first part consists of stories about the mothers, narrated by the mothers. The episodes of the second part are narrated by the daughters, describing their childhood daughter-mother relationships. The daughters also narrate the third part, discussing their adult experiences haunted by the influence of their mother-daughter relationships. The episodes in the final part are told by or about the mothers. Structurally, *The Joy Luck Club* is almost mathematical in its intricate symmetry. However, this symmetry is subtly nonlinear, for the narrative strands crisscross and flash back through time, intersecting characters, events, and recurrent imagery and symbolism.

SOURCES FOR FURTHER STUDY

Hamilton, Patricia L. "*Feng Shui*, Astrology, and the Five Elements: Traditional Chinese Belief in Amy Tan's *The Joy Luck Club*." *MELUS* 24, no. 2 (1999): 125–145.

Ho, Wendy. "Swan-Feather Mothers and Coca-Cola Daughters: Teaching Tan's *The Joy Luck Club*." In *Teaching American Ethnic Literatures*, edited by John Maitino and David Peck. Albuquerque: University of New Mexico Press, 1996.

Xu, Ben. "Memory and the Ethnic Self: Reading Amy Tan's *The Joy Luck Club*." In *Memory, Narrative, and Identity in Ethnic American Literatures*, edited by Amritjit Singh, Joseph T. Skerrett, Jr., and Robert E. Hogan. Boston: Northeastern University Press, 1994.

THE KITCHEN GOD'S WIFE

Genre: Novel
Subgenre: Feminist adventure
Published: New York, 1991
Time period: 1920s to 1960s
Setting: China; San Francisco Bay Area, California

Themes and Issues. As in its predecessor, the leading themes in *The Kitchen God's Wife* are mother-daughter miscommunication and women's empowerment and individuation. These themes are again developed through a dramatic action of suffering and survival within a Chinese landscape.

In Pellegrino Tibaldi's *Ulysses and His Companions on the Island of Cyclops* (Palazzo Poggi, Bologna, Italy), the famed wanderer attempts to flee the monster, just as Weili must escape her brutish husband. *The Kitchen God's Wife* is rich in allusions to Homer's *Odyssey*. The arc of Kwan and Olivia's journey lends the novel an epic quality.

Communication difficulties occur on several levels. Linguistically, these difficulties highlight the generational differences between the immigrant and the native-born Chinese Americans and are often tragicomic. For example, when the daughter Pearl says "beach," her mother Weili hears "bitch." Such amusing misunderstandings, however, indicate more serious problems.

As the novel begins, mother-daughter miscommunications have hardened around major secrets between Weili and Pearl that have poisoned their relationship. Pearl's secret is her multiple sclerosis. Weili's is her fear that Pearl is the child not of her loving second husband, Jimmy Louie, but of her heinous first husband, Wen Fu, who raped Weili the week before her second marriage. Once mother and daughter are able to reveal their secrets, catharsis and reconciliation occur.

Weili's narrative is a gripping *Bildungsroman*, or coming-of-age novel, reflecting Tan's common themes of women's individuation and empowerment. Weili is a girl with feelings of low self-worth who grows into a woman capable of asserting her choice of a husband at gunpoint.

The Plot. The novel consists of two narratives, Pearl's one-hundred-page narrative and Weili's three-hundred-page one. Pearl's story, dealing with mother-daughter miscommunication, frames the book, both beginning and ending it. Weili's story forms the book's substance, dealing with women's individuation and empowerment.

After growing up as a motherless daughter of a wealthy family in 1920s China, Weili gratefully marries Wen Fu, her family's choice of husband. She quickly discovers, however, that Wen Fu is a selfish and abusive sexual pervert. He cheats, squanders Weili's dowry, gambles, rapes a servant who dies attempting an abortion, beds a mistress in Weili's room, and beats his infant into retardation and death. After crashing a jeep that he bought with Weili's money, Wen Fu loses an eye and visibly takes on his true aspect, that of a Cyclops.

During this marriage, Weili endures the many woes but also grows in awareness and assertiveness, choosing to abort her pregnancies by Wen Fu. She eventually meets and falls in love with Jimmy Louie, a considerate and loving Chinese American interpreter with the American forces in China. To exercise her choice of a new husband, she empowers herself with cunning and force, the same instruments habitually employed against her. She tricks Wen Fu into signing their divorce papers, then uses his own revolver to extricate from him her airplane ticket to the United States. Thus Weili grows from a marginalized girl with no esteem and few options into a self-empowered woman who chooses which child to bear and which man to marry.

Analysis. Into this account of Weili's growth, Tan infuses several epic archetypes. For instance, the narrative, like that of Homer's *Odyssey* (c. 800 B.C.E.), is about the sufferings endured in a lengthy wartime journey. Another allusion to Homeric archetype is Tan's one-eyed Wen Fu, who mirrors the giant Cyclops of Greek myth. The adventures of both Homer's and Tan's protagonists occur under the auspices of female deities: Pallas Athena and the Kitchen God's Wife. Furthermore, the beginning of Tan's novel resembles the beginning of Homer's epic; both commence through the rather slow-moving narrative of a child—Tan's Pearl and Homer's Telemachus—seeking an exciting, much-traveled parent. Both works also conclude with their protagonists' reestablishment of hearth and home—Odysseus in his original Ithaca, Weili in her New World California. Such parallels, fortuitous or not, point up the universal qualities and broad appeal of Tan's novel.

SOURCES FOR FURTHER STUDY

Caesar, Judith. "Patriarchy, Imperialism, and Knowledge in *The Kitchen God's Wife*." *North Dakota Quarterly* 62, no. 4 (1994): 164–174.

Ong, Caroline. "Re-Writing the Old Wives Tales." *Times Literary Supplement*, July 5, 1991, p. 20.

Tan, Amy. "Angst and the Second Novel." *Publisher's Weekly* 238 (April 5, 1991): 1–4.

Other Works

THE CHINESE SIAMESE CAT (1994). This children's book, illustrated by Gretchen Shields, is calculated to encourage pride in one's ethnic origins, to praise instigators of social change, and to promote the values of joy and artistic expression over those of inhibition and societal repression.

A mother Siamese cat decides to tell her kittens why their tails are black. Their ancestors were Chinese cats who belonged to a Chinese Foolish Magistrate. The Magistrate wrote his strict laws with the tails of his cats dipped in ink—hence the cats' dark tails. One day, one mischievous kitten tumbled into the ink, walked on the papers, and blotted out all the negative words in the Magistrate's laws.

When these altered edicts were proclaimed, there was an outbreak of joy, individuality, and artistic expression. Society was changed—and, unexpectedly, so was the Magistrate, who found that he liked his fellow citizens better as joyful individuals capable of harmonious expression in song. Therefore, concludes Mother Cat, her kittens have reason to take pride in their ethnic ancestors and in their own dark tails, because their ancestors helped to bring about positive social change, promoted joyfulness and creativity, and taught a foolish man wisdom.

THE HUNDRED SECRET SENSES (1995). Amy Tan's third novel was greeted with mixed reviews. It departs from the mother-daughter focus of Tan's previous long fiction and focuses on sisterly relationships. The two narrator-protagonists are Chinese American half-sisters living in San Francisco. The elder, Kwan, is an immigrant from China; the younger, Olivia, is a part-Caucasian born in the United States. Olivia is a rather unremarkable young, urban professional photojournalist whose seventeen-year marriage to Simon, a freelance writer, is ending.

Tan has created for Kwan, however, the remarkable gift of *yin* eyes, which enable Kwan to communicate with the dead and recall previous existences. Whereas the art of *feng shui* permeates the worldview of *The Joy Luck Club*, notions about reincarnation and karma undergird *The Hundred Secret Senses*. Tan mingles this Asian supernaturalism with American realism to concoct an intriguing Asian American brand of Magical Realism, a genre popularized by Gabriel García Márquez in his novel *One Hundred Years of Solitude* (1967).

Kwan can see Simon's dead fiancé, whose memory still troubles Olivia. She also remembers her previous incarnation as Nunumu, during the 1851–1864 Taiping Rebellion in China, a populist revolt against the Manchurian Ch'ing Dynasty that ultimately cost over twenty million lives. The rebellion was led by Hung Hsiu-ch'üan, a member of the oppressed Hakka minority, who claimed to be Jesus Christ's younger brother. Nunumu is a Hakka, too, and a servant and friend of a Christian missionary, Miss Banner, who is currently reincarnated as Olivia. Miss Banner has an affair with General Cape, a treacherous mercenary, though her true love is the interpreter, Yiban, currently reincarnated as Simon. Nunumu tries to steer Miss Banner toward her true love, but her scheme fails, and they all lose their lives.

In her current reincarnation, therefore, Kwan is trying to improve Olivia's karma, first by enabling Simon to propose and then by trying to mend Olivia's troubled marriage. In her attempts at the latter, Kwan brings the couple to the Chinese village of their former incarnations, where, during an unplanned morning dalliance, Olivia becomes impregnated by Simon, who supposedly had been sterile. Kwan then disappears into the neighborhood caves and is presumed dead. Olivia and Simon return to California, where they remain separated but live fairly happily together on weekends.

THE MOON LADY (1992). This children's book, illustrated by Gretchen Shields, has the same protagonist and story line as "The Moon

Lady" episode in *The Joy Luck Club* but a more toned-down vocabulary and a more naïve narrative perspective. The theme in both versions is equally profound: the loss and recovery of the self. Both versions also allude to the Chinese myth of the Moon Goddess who, Eve-like, asserts her self-worth by stealing her husband's Peach of Immortality and absconding to the moon.

Ying-ying is a seven-year-old girl from a wealthy family in China. During a harvest Moon Festival outing on the lake, Ying-ying falls into the water and is lost. While missing, she is mistaken for a vagabond girl, and she glimpses an opera featuring the Moon Lady, who grants secret wishes. When Ying-ying ventures backstage to make a wish, she discovers that the Moon Lady is really a male actor. Shocked, she runs away—into the arms of her searching family. She realizes that her secret wish is to be found by her family and, by implication, to banish questions of identity and gender roles.

Resources

Many resources on Amy Tan can be found on the World Wide Web. Also, most of Tan's books are available on audiocassette. Sources of information for students of Amy Tan include the following:

Anniina's Amy Tan Page. A fairly extensive on-line resource on Amy Tan is Anniina's Amy Tan Page. It includes links to on-line reviews and criticism, interviews, and audio and video recordings. (http://www.luminarium.org/contemporary/amytan/)

The *Salon* Interview. The on-line magazine *Salon* interviewed Tan in November 1995. The discussion is posted on the World Wide Web. (http://www.salon.com/12nov1995/feature/tan.html)

Book Reviews. Excerpts of reviews of *The Joy Luck Club* are found on the Web at The Joy Luck Club home page (and Anniina's Amy Tan Page, mentioned above), along with biographical information, analysis, and suggested reading on women's issues and culturally diverse books. Links to diverse sites about Asia are also included. (http://www.cwrl.utexas.edu/~sbowen/314fall/novels/).

Video Recording. A video of the Rock Bottom Remainders, the band in which Tan, Stephen King, Dave Barry, and others play, was filmed in 1993 and is available from BMG Video.

C. L. CHUA

Studs Terkel

BORN: May 16, 1912, New York, New York
IDENTIFICATION: Late-twentieth-century radio host known for his popular oral histories on a range of topics at the center of twentieth-century American life.

Throughout the latter half of the twentieth century, Studs Terkel captured the pulse of the American people in a dozen different books that arguably can be collectively called America's memory book. He interviewed thousands of men and women, old and young, about their work, about their memories of America's past, and about their hopes for the future, compiling the best of this testimony in his many volumes of oral history. His conversations with people, both famous and unknown, reveal his subjects' true feelings about themselves and their country, at the same time revealing the heart and soul of the United States in the twentieth century.

The Writer's Life

Louis "Studs" Terkel was born on May 16, 1912, in the Bronx borough of New York, to Samuel and Anna Terkel, Jewish immigrants from Russia. Nine years later, his parents moved Terkel and his two older brothers, Meyer and Ben, to Chicago, where they managed and lived in hotels.

Childhood. Although Terkel's parents lost nearly all their assets in the stock market crash of 1929, Terkel managed to continue his education. At the age of sixteen he entered the University of Chicago. After graduating four years later, he continued at the university, pursuing a law degree, which he received in 1934 and never used professionally.

Early Work in Radio. During the late 1930s, Terkel held a number of jobs, working for the Federal Writers' Project and acting and writing for the radio. After a brief tour in the U.S. Army, he established himself in radio in Chicago as both writer and performer in 1945. As a folk-music disc jockey, he helped make popular the gospel singer Mahalia Jackson, with whom he remained friends until her death in 1972. On the basis of his radio work, Terkel became a music critic for a Chicago newspaper. In 1950 he began hosting *Studs' Place,* a television show that ran for three years in the "golden" years of early television and was a fresh and open mixture of folk music and stimulating talk.

This period of Terkel's career ended in the early 1950s, with the anticommunist blacklist of Senator Joseph McCarthy, which banned certain performers from film and television work because of their alleged political activities in the 1930s. Terkel was never bitter about the blacklist, however, because it forced him back into radio, which was the better medium for his many talents. Indeed, Mahalia Jackson soon signed him on as a writer for her radio show.

In 1954 Terkel joined WFMT, a small Chicago radio station that allowed him the freedom to explore his various interests. He worked there for the next forty-five years, playing mostly jazz and blues

Pianist Chet Roble (left) and Terkel rehearse the music for an episode of *Studs' Place,* Terkel's human-interest television show that aired on Friday nights in the early 1950s.

Terkel stands with President and Mrs. Clinton on the South Lawn of the White House after being presented with the National Book Foundation Medal in September 1997.

music and interviewing first the artists who made it, and then an increasingly larger circle of people, famous, infamous, and unknown. In addition to his daily radio work, Terkel also found time to write plays, such as *Amazing Grace,* produced in 1959; to produce records, such as *Born to Live: Hiroshima* (1961); and to host live jazz and folk concerts, such as the Newport Jazz Festival, in 1959 and 1960.

Publishing. Terkel's first book, *Giants of Jazz* (1957), came directly out of his radio music work, as his later books would come out of his radio interviews. The first of these, *Division Street: America* (1967), was inspired by Andre Schiffrin, an editor at Pantheon who commissioned Terkel to interview people about their native city of Chicago. At the age of forty-five, Terkel began a new career. Most of his books were inspired by discussions with Schiffrin and

were published by Pantheon, and Terkel acknowledged the help of his friend and publisher in every book. Over the next three decades, Terkel addressed some of the toughest topics in American life—the Great Depression, the American Dream, World War II, the world of work, the American obsession with race—and he would get people from all walks of life to speak openly and honestly about these topics.

Later Years. Terkel continued in his many capacities throughout the 1990s. He hosted a radio show until 1997; he conducted and collected his interviews into a series of volumes on a number of important topics; and he even kept up his acting career, playing a journalist in *Eight Men Out* (1988), John Sayles's film about the Chicago "Black Sox" baseball scandal of 1919.

Some of Terkel's best work reflects his long-standing love affair with Chicago, seen here in 1955. It formed a vibrant back-drop to his roving interviews in which he plumbed the thoughts and feelings of the city's diverse residents.

Terkel has won both popular and critical acclaim for his many volumes of interviews and has been recognized as a landmark in American literature. In 1997 he was awarded the National Book Foundation Medal for distinguished contribution to American letters. A talkative interviewer, Terkel has rarely given personal interviews, remaining rather closed about certain parts of his own life. His autobiographical *Talking to Myself: A Memoir of My Times* (1977) was much more about his times than his life. Unlike many other famous American writers, Terkel has remained in his hometown and in his long marriage and has continued to do the work he loves.

NONFICTION

1957   Giants of Jazz

1967   Division Street: America

1970   Hard Times: An Oral History of the Great Depression in America

1974   Working: People Talk About What They Do All Day and How They Feel About What They Do

1977   Talking to Myself: A Memoir of My Times

1980   American Dreams: Lost and Found

1984   "The Good War": An Oral History of World War II

1986   Chicago

1988   The Great Divide: Second Thoughts on the American Dream

1992   Race: How Blacks and Whites Think and Feel About the American Obsession

1995   Coming of Age: The Story of Our Century by Those Who've Lived It

1997   My American Century

1999   The Spectator: Talk About Movies and Plays with Those Who Make Them

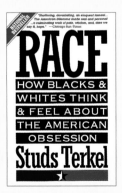

HIGHLIGHTS IN
TERKEL'S LIFE

1912   Louis "Studs" Terkel is born in the Bronx borough of New York on May 16.

1921   Moves to Chicago with parents and two brothers.

1932   Graduates from the University of Chicago.

1934   Receives his law degree from the University of Chicago.

1934   Works throughout the decade as Chicago radio and stage actor.

1939   Marries Ida Goldberg.

1942   Serves for a year in the U.S. Army as a troop entertainer.

1943   Begins working as Chicago radio newscaster and disc jockey.

1950   Begins hosting the nationally televised show *Studs' Place.*

1953   Leaves television after being blacklisted by Senator Joseph McCarthy's anti-communist campaign.

1954   Begins hosting *The Studs Terkel Show* on WFMT radio station in Chicago.

1957   Publishes *Giants of Jazz.*

1967   Publishes *Division Street: America.*

1970   Publishes *Hard Times: An Oral History of the Great Depression in America.*

1974   Publishes *Working: People Talk About What They Do All Day and How They Feel About What They Do.*

1977   Publishes *Talking to Myself: A Memoir of My Times.*

1980   Publishes *American Dreams: Lost and Found.*

1985   Wins Pulitzer Prize for *"The Good War": An Oral History of World War II* (1984).

1986   Publishes *Chicago.*

1988   Publishes *The Great Divide: Second Thoughts on the American Dream.*

1992   Publishes *Race: How Blacks and Whites Think and Feel About the American Obsession.*

1995   Publishes *Coming of Age: The Story of Our Century by Those Who've Lived It.*

1997   Wins the National Book Foundation Medal for distinguished contribution to American letters.

1999   Publishes *The Spectator: Talk About Movies and Plays with Those Who Make Them.*

Many of Studs Terkel's interviews began in the radio studios in Chicago, where for decades he was a radio host. Although he has spoken with many important and successful people over the years, most of his subjects have been articulate working-class or blue-collar citizens who can explain their lives in terms all listeners and readers can understand. His gift is the ability to weave these interviews into thoughtful memory tapestries for the general reading public.

Terkel and Oral History. Terkel's work, like his reputation, falls outside the borders of traditional literature. His work consists not so much of his own writing as of his skill of interviewing interesting people and editing their words. This particular form of history writing came of age during the period in which Terkel was producing his collections of interviews—in part because of his work. There are now numerous resources in this field.

Terkel's Literary Beginnings. Terkel produced radio interviews for several years before attempting his first book, *Giants of Jazz,* in 1957. The book is a portrait of thirteen jazz musicians, from Louis Armstrong and Bessie Smith to Stan Kenton and Dizzy Gillespie, and has been reprinted several times, even in illustrated editions for children.

Terkel's first book in the oral history genre that made him famous was *Division Street: America,* published in 1967. Set in Chicago, the work collects "the thoughts of noncelebrated people . . . concerning themselves, past and present, the city, the society, the world." This "cross-section of urban thought" demonstrated that most people at the end of the 1960s

were thinking about civil rights and Vietnam. The book also demonstrated that Terkel did not so much interview people as listen to them talk.

People and Issues in Terkel's Work.
Terkel's fame was established over the next fifteen years, with *Hard Times: An Oral History of the Great Depression in America; Working: People Talk About What They Do All Day and How They Feel About What They Do; American Dreams: Lost and Found; and "The Good War": An Oral History of World War II,* capped by his winning

Diana Ong's painting *America* reflects varied interview subjects Terkel came across in his years of listening to the many voices of America. Instead of interviewing the celebrated or the privileged, he sought out average citizens. His respect for his subjects was rewarded with a trove of frank and heartfelt responses.

the Pulitzer Prize for history. These four volumes established, and later collections confirmed, the range and depth of Terkel's focus. Terkel looks at difficult subjects in American history, subjects that many people had some difficulty discussing: the Great Depression, World War II, race relations, and work. In the cumulative body of his work, Terkel has provided a collective portrait of Americans at the end of the twentieth century and of their feelings about themselves, about their past and their future, about each other, and about their country.

Methodology in Terkel's Work.

At the same time, reviewers and historians have complained about the loose structure of Terkel's methodology. Nowhere in the prefaces and introductions to his many books does Terkel lay out his method; rather, he says only that he has relied on a tape recorder and that his editors have played an important part in all his work. How he found his subjects, how much was cut out of his interviews and how much was added, what questions he asked to prompt the responses—these and other important issues remain unanswered. He was trained not as a historian, but as a live radio interviewer, and he continued that style in his writing.

Critics complain about Terkel's lack of objectivity and whether the informants in *Hard Times,* for example, are the most representative. Terkel has also relied heavily on certain people for his interviews: Peggy Terry appears in four of his books, film critic Pauline Kael is in three, and a number of others show up twice. Finally, Terkel's own biases may influence his choice of interview subjects, and cer-

Terkel's subjects express an abiding love for their country as well as dismay and disillusion, as with these World War I veterans who gathered in Washington, D.C., in 1932. Their sign reads, "We have come to collect the gratitude that was promised us for participating in the World War."

tainly the ways in which he edits their interviews for final publication. Another subjective factor in Terkel's work is his progressive social agenda, which is clear from the titles of his books and may subjectively affect the editing of his interviews.

All these complaints about Terkel's methods may be moot because his interviews reveal how good Terkel is at what he does. He has the uncanny knack not only to get people talking but also to listen in such a way that they reveal themselves candidly, confessing their innermost thoughts and fears. He uses these revelations to build the books for which he is famous, books that give voice to the underlying American spirit.

In his later works, Terkel has become somewhat more pessimistic, as these books reveal a United States still unable to realize its dreams of racial equality and social justice. *The Great Divide: Second Thoughts on the American Dream* and *Race: How Blacks and Whites Think and Feel About the American Obsession* in particular demonstrate that the American determination that carried the country through the Great Depression and World War II may finally be unable to bring about the society that Terkel and his best informants have always believed was possible.

BIBLIOGRAPHY

Baker, James Thomas. *Studs Terkel*. New York: Twayne Publishers, 1992.

Dunaway, David K., and Willa K. Baum, eds. *Oral History: An Interdisciplinary Anthology*. 2d ed. Walnut Creek, Calif.: AltaMira Press, 1996.

Frisch, Michael, ed. *A Shared Authority: Essays on the Craft and Meaning of Oral and Public History*. Albany: State University of New York Press, 1990.

Grele, Ronald J., ed. *Envelopes of Sound*. Chicago: Precedent Publishing, 1985.

Parker, Tony. *Studs Terkel: A Life in Words*. New York: Holt, 1996.

Prescott, Peter S. "Studs' Best Tapes." *Newsweek,* April 1, 1974, pp. 76–78.

Seldon, Anthony, and Joanna Pappworth. *By Word of Mouth: "Elite" Oral History*. New York: Methuen, 1983.

Stern, Richard. "Studs Terkel." *The Antioch Review* 53 (Fall 1995): 454.

Terkel, Studs. *Talking to Myself: A Memoir of My Times*. New York: Pantheon, 1977.

The blank faces bereft of hope reflect the pessimism of Terkel's later works. Men stand around and wait for better times in Ben Shahn's painting *Unemployment*.

The Spectator: Talk about Movies and Plays with Those Who Make Them

Genre: Nonfiction
Subgenre: Oral history
Published: New York, 1999
Time period: 1950s–1990s
Setting: The United States

Themes and Issues. Studs Terkel's most recent volume of interviews returns to his first love: theatre and film. Culled from his forty-five years as a daily radio host in Chicago, *The Spectator* collects fifty interviews Terkel conducted with actors and actresses, directors, playwrights, critics, and others associated with the performing arts.

The Spectator resembles Terkel's 1974 *Working* in its focus on craft and trade, but it differs from that earlier work—and in fact from any of Terkel's dozen other books—by being devoted to those whose names have lit up marquees around the world. In *The Spectator,* in short, Terkel has given up his usual focus on the common man and given in to his fans' love of film and theater.

Terkel actually began his own long career as a performer, in Chicago radio drama in the 1930s. He appeared occasionally after that on television and in films (he played a journalist in *Eight Men Out* in 1988, for example), and it is clear he never lost his love for the stage and film. *The Spectator* allows readers to share his curiosity about how plays and movies are created, and to learn how their crafts—of writing, directing, acting—are practiced.

The Interviews. The interviews in *The Spectator* range from the 1950s to the 1990s. Along the way Terkel interviews such notable artists and performers as actor Hal Holbrook, playwright Lorraine Hansberry, comedian Moms Mabley, Italian film director Federico Fellini, writer William Saroyan, actor Ian McKellen, and playwright August Wilson.

Terkel on the air in Chicago on April 15, 1977, just days before the publication of his memoir, *Talking to Myself*, in which he writes about both famous and everyday people he met.

Some of the best interviews took place over some years: Terkel interviewed actor Zero Mostel in both 1961 and 1976; playwright Tennessee Williams in 1961 and 1981; puppeteer Burr Tillstrom in 1966 and 1978; and playwright Edward Albee in 1968 and 1995. Such double interviews often reveal the growth and development of an artist's career.

A number of the interviews were originally done for earlier Terkel collections: Three interviews—with the stage director Jack Kirkland, the actor Hiram Sherman, and the lyricist E. Y. Harburg—are from *Hard Times*. The interview with stage director Joan Littlewood originally appeared in *Talking to Myself;* the interview with Arnold Schwarzenegger originally appeared in *American Dreams*. Terkel conducted the interview with *The New Yorker* film critic Pauline Kael for *"The Good War"* in 1984.

The Spectator has a number of openings. In the introduction, historian Garry Wills calls this Terkel's best book. In the section entitled "Overture," Terkel himself reminisces about his career and describes in great detail the plays and films of the 1920s and 1930s that created his tastes. In "Prologue: Morning, Noon, and Night," which contains a brief interview with Kirkland from *Hard Times*, Terkel reiterates the influence that the lively arts have had on his life and on his career.

The interviews that follow are divided into three acts and numerous scenes, or subjects, in each act: ways of doing/seeing, winners and losers, and others. *The Spectator* takes film and theatergoers behind the scenes to show how the illusions are created and maintained. Terkel has a fan's fascination with the glamour and mystery but is also a thoughtful interviewer who has done his homework, getting his respondents to talk openly about their work.

Terkel is aided by the fact that the people he interviews are bright and articulate. The interviews with British theater directors Peter Hall and Jonathan Miller,

Terkel's growing success as a broadcaster allowed him to showcase a variety of actors and musicians alike. Here, Terkel (far left) sits in with, from left to right, country blues singers Win Stracke, Big Bill Broonzy, and Larry Lane around 1950.

The skyline of Chicago, Terkel's beloved city.

for example, are mini-courses on the history of theater and the nature of the theatrical experience. The actresses Ruth Gordon and Geraldine Page give Terkel seminars on performance, while critics Kenneth Tynan and Pauline Kael dissect theater and film, respectively. Agnes De Mille describes to Terkel the enormous work it takes to be a dancer and choreographer in America, and Eva La Gallienne, director of the National Repertory Theater in 1964, gives Terkel a lecture on drama. James Cagney, interviewed in 1981 after he had returned to film in *Ragtime* (1981), provides a meditation on aging and creativity; Lila Kedrova, who acted in *Zorba the Greek* (1964), among other films, does a meditation on death. Marlon Brando turns the tables on Terkel and interviews the interviewer with enlightening results.

Analysis. Terkel draws from his subjects their essential thoughts and feelings about their work, getting them to reveal the relation between their art and the larger world of work and politics and prompting them to speculate on the meaning of their craft to the world. These interviews mostly have the feel of interesting conversations on how plays and films get made with the people who do them. In one of a number of amusing stories in the collection, Terkel tells about weeping at the performance of Paul Lukas in the 1930s play *Watch on the Rhine*, only to find out after the play that Lukas was playing to an attractive young woman "in the third row to the left." It is always fascinating to read what is really going on beyond the stage and behind the screen.

SOURCES FOR FURTHER STUDY

Dunaway, David K., and Willa K. Baum, eds. *Oral History: An Interdisciplinary Anthology.* 2d ed. Walnut Creek, Calif.: AltaMira Press, 1996.

Parker, Tony. *Studs Terkel: A Life in Words.* New York: Holt, 1996.

Terkel, Studs. *Talking to Myself: A Memoir of My Times.* New York: Pantheon, 1977.

SOME INSPIRATIONS BEHIND TERKEL'S WORK

Studs Terkel has been influenced by a broad range of models, only a few of them literary. One of his heroes was the Progressive Party's candidate for president in 1924, Robert "Battling Bob" La Follette, who won nearly five million votes. La Follette represented to Terkel—as did the union leader Eugene Debs and the lawyer Clarence Darrow—the underdog who fights for average people.

Terkel's first work of oral history, *Division Street: America,* was dedicated to the architect Louis Sullivan, who pioneered the tall office building and transformed the Chicago skyline; the social reformer Jane Addams, who founded Hull House, an early settlement house in Chicago; and the 1920s sports journalist and short-story writer Ring Lardner. These three people represent a good sense of Terkel's models.

Terkel was likewise clearly influenced by twentieth-century American social writers such as Chicago novelist James T. Farrell, from whose protagonist, Studs Lonigan, Terkel takes his nickname, and his friend Nelson Algren, the author of gritty, realistic Chicago novels such as *The Man with the Golden Arm* (1949) and *A Walk on the Wild Side* (1956). Terkel is in the clear line of the American writers and social activists of the 1920s and after, and of radical journalists such as I. F. Stone and A. J. Liebling. His interview style may have been influenced by the oral history work he did with the Federal Writers' Project in the late 1930s.

Terkel also clearly has been affected by the work of the musicians whom he has played with, interviewed, and written about for decades. He often mentions the country blues player Big Bill Broonzy and Mahalia Jackson. These artists, like the best subjects in his books, touch upon some of the deeper themes in American life and also represent an ideal, integrated society, where citizens of every color can enjoy music and life unhindered by social rules and restrictions. Finally, the jazz form is clearly an influence on the improvisational mode and direction of many of Terkel's interviews. In a way, Terkel's best interviews are themselves jazz performances. The inspirations behind Terkel's work, in short, are nontraditional and come from a range of forms— musical, literary, and social. Careful readers can find in his books the echoes of some of the outstanding historical and cultural figures of the twentieth century.

Big Bill Broonzy, seen here in 1957, was born into a Mississippi sharecropping family. Not only did he come to inspire Terkel, he influenced many young blues musicians as well, often taking artists under his wing and helping them secure recording sessions and performance dates.

Reader's Guide to Major Works

AMERICAN DREAMS: LOST AND FOUND

Genre: Nonfiction
Subgenre: Oral history
Published: New York, 1980
Time period: Twentieth century
Setting: United States

Themes and Issues. Unlike most of Studs Terkel's other collections of interviews—*Hard Times* or *"The Good War,"* for example—*American Dreams: Lost and Found* is built not on an idea, but on a time period. Although the volume has a more vague focus than Terkel's previous books, the volume ends up being one of Terkel's most interesting, because the American Dream is such a central concept to American culture. "In this book are a hundred American voices," Terkel writes in his introduction, "captured by hunch, circumstance, and a rough idea. There is no pretense at statistical 'truth,' nor consensus. There is, in the manner of a jazz work, an attempt, of theme and improvisation, to recount dreams, lost and found, and a recognition of possibility." The volume is like other Terkel studies, more a memory book than a formal history, but it marks the turning point in his own historically optimistic view of the American future.

The Interviews. The tone of the book can be found in the two conversations that make up the prologue and in the two that comprise the epilogue. The volume opens with "Miss U.S.A.," a graphic description of a young woman's disillusionment after winning the pageant of the chapter's title. It is followed by the story of Leonel I. Castillo, the former director of the federal Immigration and Naturalization Service (INS) and a third-generation Mexican immigrant, who talks about how the same dream that fueled immigration for centuries is still alive in America: "They want to share in the American dream. The Stream never ends."

The epilogue includes the stories of an Oregon logger, who rhapsodizes about the beauty of the remaining American wilderness and warns of the multiple threats against it, and the son of a slave on the way to the August 25, 1963, March on Washington, who tells Terkel how proud he is to be a part of the fight for civil rights. In between these two sets of interviews are the dreams, lost and found, of people who have sought success in America. As the prologue and epilogue make clear, there are more dashed hopes and broken promises than fulfilled dreams.

One clear theme in *American Dreams* is the myth of the hero in books by Horatio Alger, the late-nineteenth-century writer whose characters went from rags to riches. *American Dreams* reveals the stories of people, such as Ted Turner and Arnold Schwarzenegger, who have actually raised themselves "by their bootstraps," and have gone from rags to riches. The book describes how power operates in the United States, and who actually has it. The book also shows that, for some people at least, the American Dream is still a reality, regularly reinforced by Hollywood images. *American Dreams* also tellingly hints at the gaps in American life—between the old and the young, between the haves and the have-nots, and between those on different sides of the racial divide.

Analysis. If *American Dreams* expresses an optimism about the state of life in the United States, Terkel's follow-up volume, *The Great Divide: Second Thoughts on the American Dream,* published eight years later, reflects a modified view only hinted at in the previous volume. "I wanted to show how things have changed," Terkel told an interviewer, "between one generation and the next, maybe perhaps let's say within two generations." The later work is less optimistic than its predecessor; Terkel is struck, after eight years of the Ronald Reagan

In *American Dreams: Lost and Found,* an Oregon logger waxes poetic about the beauties of the American wilderness, the lush solitude captured in Albert Bierstadt's painting *Cathedral Forest. American Dreams* is a loose collection of interviews, which form a more impromptu, free-flowing narrative.

presidency, by the total lack of historical memory in the United States. Citizens do not seem to remember who they are, where they came from, and of what they are capable.

The divide includes the growing gap between wealth and poverty in America: The week that Forbes magazine "announced that the number of billionaires had doubled in the past year . . . Shasta County, California, closed its entire library system for lack of funds." Terkel also notes the racial gap in the United States, which he would explore more fully in *Race: How Blacks and Whites Think and Feel About the American Obsession*.

Another gap exists between those who remember the Depression, World War II, the Civil Rights movement—and what good came out of these struggles—and those who have been numbed by popular culture and do not remember much of America's past. *The Great Divide* is an even more pessimistic work than *American Dreams*. In less than a decade, Terkel's informants have lost some of their hope for America, and for the American Dream.

SOURCES FOR FURTHER STUDY

Brashler, William. "Touring America's Streets of Dreams with Studs Terkel." *Chicago Tribune,* September 14, 1980, pp. 7–1, 7–5.

Stern, Richard. "Studs Terkel." *The Antioch Review* 53 (Fall 1995): 454.

West, Hollie. "Talking Terkel." *The Washington Post,* November 27, 1980, p. C1.

HARD TIMES: AN ORAL HISTORY OF THE GREAT DEPRESSION IN AMERICA

Genre: Nonfiction
Subgenre: Oral history
Published: New York, 1970
Time period: 1930s
Setting: United States, particularly Chicago and the Midwest

Themes and Issues. An immediate best-seller when it was published in 1970, *Hard Times* remained on the *New York Times* best-seller list for over five months and was even more popu-

lar when it was published as a paperback the following year. There is no introduction to this oral history of the great depression, but in "A Personal Memoir *(and parenthetical comment)*" that opens the volume, Terkel calls *Hard Times* "a memory book, rather than one of hard fact and precise statistic." The book includes interviews with 166 people over 529 pages in what Terkel says is "an attempt to get the story of the holocaust known as the Great Depression from an improvised battalion of survivors," from the famous, such as farm labor leader César Chavez, to the infamous, such as fan dancer Sally Rand, with many average Americans in between.

The Interviews. For the serious student of history, *Hard Times* poses several problems. First, Terkel does not explain how or when the interviews were chosen and conducted, the plan by which the volume was organized into five books and more than thirty subsections, or his principles in editing individual interviews. Although many of the interviews are introduced, giving a brief background and personal history of the informants, Terkel rarely tells readers how he met the interviewers. He also does not inform readers that most of the people are from Chicago and the Midwest, where a severe Depression-era drought particularly affected that area. The framework and methodology of *Hard Times* are thus loose and vague. It is the focus on the Great Depression that gives *Hard Times* its unity and holds it together as well as it does.

Despite these limitations, *Hard Times* is one of the best accounts of the 1930s for general readers, reflecting the diversity of 1930s life and the great swarm of incidents, ideas, and feelings that defined that complex period. Terkel's informants represent the decade's social range: ex-hoboes, farmers, financiers, entertainers, miners, business leaders, unionists, writers, and social workers.

The stories are on the whole fascinating to read, and they illustrate, in great detail, every aspect of Depression life. Some people experienced the 1930s as grimly as characters from the period's proletarian novels; others lived through the

Hard Times: An Oral History of the Great Depression in America recounts the devastation of the period. In this photograph, a hungry group lines up in Detroit in 1930 for a meager meal of bread and soup.

decade unaware that a depression was going on; some, in 1970, are unaware that the Depression has ended. The interviewers talk to Terkel about hopping freight trains across the country and about joining the 1932 Bonus March of unemployed veterans on Washington, D.C.; about lynch mobs and people they knew who jumped from windows out of financial desperation; about strikes and migrant labor camps.

What strikes the reader most forcefully about Terkel's book is that, for the majority of its respondents, the Depression was a good time as much as it was a hard time. People remember and talk about the suffering and the violence, but these difficulties are more than balanced by their memories of the hope and excitement of the period, by the camaraderie and social unity, by the shared sense of achievement and adventure. Life was important then, one informant says—life was significant. That was a very free and happy period, another reports. All in all, another concludes, it was a painful time, but a glorious time.

As Terkel summarizes this theme in his preface, "Perhaps it was the best of times. Or was it the worst?" Apparently it was both. As difficult as the Great Depression was, people remember their shared struggles positively. When people in *Hard Times* try to fix blame for the economic and social problems of the decade, they tend to blame themselves. As Terkel notes in his preface, there is "a private kind of shame" and "a personal guilt" about the events of the 1930s.

At the same time that readers catch the complexity and even contradiction in *Hard Times,* they may sense that a price is being paid against the present. It was a decade of involvement, one person says of the 1930s. "It's a cold world now. It was a hot world then." In the most concrete expression of this mood: "I think the Depression had some kind of human qualities that we lack now." In short, the decade of the 1930s looks better from the perspective of the late 1960s. There is more hatred and more apathy now, informants tell Terkel; people are softer than they were in the 1930s and less generous; and they do not want to work anymore.

Terkel finally asks what would happen if there were a depression today. The overwhelming response: the nation would never make it through, people would not survive; there would be a dictatorship, there would be a revolution. "When I was sixteen, I wasn't afraid to die," warns one man. "But the kid, sixteen now, is not afraid to kill."

Analysis. Since Terkel's book was released, a number of serious studies of the Great Depression have been published, but none have replaced the fresh and personal testimony of *Hard Times,* and there still is no better general introduction to the informal social history of the period or better account of what it actually felt like to live through the Depression. Like most of Terkel's other books, *Hard Times* takes readers inside history through firsthand accounts of what it was like to live at that time.

SOURCES FOR FURTHER STUDY

Frisch, Michael, ed. "Oral History and Hard Times: A Review Essay." In *A Shared Authority: Essays on the Craft and Meaning of Oral and Public History.* Albany: State University of New York Press, 1990.

Stern, Richard. "Studs Terkel." *The Antioch Review* 53 (Fall 1995): 454.

West, Hollie. "Talking Terkel." *The Washington Post,* November 27, 1980, p. C1.

WORKING: PEOPLE TALK ABOUT WHAT THEY DO ALL DAY AND HOW THEY FEEL ABOUT WHAT THEY DO

Genre: Nonfiction
Subgenre: Oral history
Published: New York, 1974
Time period: Twentieth century
Setting: United States

Themes and Issues. By most accounts, *Working* is one of the best interview collections in Terkel's long and prolific career. Another instant best-seller, the volume sold over one million copies in hardcover and paperback in the quarter-century after its original publica-

tion. The volume contains 134 interviews in 589 pages, organized into 9 books: people who work the land; people who work in the communications industry; those who clean and protect property; those who work with cars; those who tend to personal needs; those who work in minor professions (pharmacy, piano tuning, etc.); those who work in the glamour industries (media, sports); entertainers, publishers and educators; and people who changed work midway through their careers and who pass their work on to their children.

Although there is a long introduction to this volume, Terkel again explains neither his editorial policy nor his method of selecting and interviewing people. In spite of its limitations, critics have universally praised *Working* for providing what few books give readers, an inside look at work, as in the book's subtitle, *People Talk About What They Do All Day and How They Feel About What They Do.* The book was so popular that it spawned a theatrical production, Stephen Schwartz's *Working: The Musical* (1978).

The Essays. Working helps to break employment stereotypes: Some of the most eloquent informants in the volume are blue-collar workers, and some of the most glamorous jobs are the least satisfying. A number of people in *Working* seem dissatisfied with their jobs, and that is especially true in the corporate world, where there is insecurity at all levels of the so-called corporate ladder. Many people with whom Terkel spoke would like to quit their jobs, but because they cannot, they sound conflicted. Everyone, however, wants to talk about their jobs, and they do so loudly in these interviews.

Analysis. One overriding issue in the book seems to be the quest for immortality, the human desire to leave something behind in one's work—be it that of a carpenter or of a corporate executive. Even more important is the quest for dignity, which is lacking in many jobs and satisfied in a few. The book is about the search, Terkel states in his introduction,

Working provides an inside look at the collective ethic that has fueled the nation's economic base. It testifies to the pride some people bring to their jobs, the power they feel in making things, such as these factory workers in William Gropper's 1941 mural *Automobile Industry* (Smithsonian American Art Museum, Washington, D.C.).

"for daily meaning as well as daily bread, for recognition as well as cash." The happiest people in the book, it appears, are people who make things: bakers, stonemasons, bookbinders. The most articulate respondents here "murmur of a hunger for 'beauty,' 'a meaning,' 'a sense of pride.'"

Working also reveals, in its publication at the beginning of the sexual revolution in the last quarter of the twentieth century, that there were many strong women in the workforce who knew exactly what they wanted from their lives and from their work. In sum, *Working*

helped to refocus attention on the importance of work in the daily lives of Americans, at a moment in cultural history when it was disappearing from the television screen and from popular culture.

SOURCES FOR FURTHER STUDY

Parker, Tony. *Studs Terkel: A Life in Words.* New York: Holt, 1996.

Peck, Abe. "Studs Terkel's New Dreams." *Rolling Stone,* July 13, 1978, pp. 8, 22.

Pfeffer, Richard M. *Working for Capitalism.* New York: Columbia University Press, 1979.

Other Works

COMING OF AGE: THE STORY OF OUR CENTURY BY THOSE WHO'VE LIVED IT

(1995). This collection is several books in one. The volume includes seventy interviews with men and women over seventy (the oldest is ninety-nine). The respondents give a panoramic view of American life through the twentieth century and show the ways in which that life

has changed for many. Among other themes, these people tell readers about how much more cold and less personal the world seems today than when they were young. In the process they also give vivid pictures of the past. The book is thus a portrait of the century by those who lived it. At the same time it is about aging and the treatment of the elderly in the United States.

Coming of Age helps articulate the sweeping changes that have gripped American society as seen through the lens of the elderly. One of Terkel's intentions in assembling the book was to show how much can be learned from the experiences and insights of the interviewees. Mary Ellen Edwards's 1887 work *The Green Leaf and the Sere* shows this continuum from age to age, from the young to the old.

Coming of Age actually serves as a kind of coda to several of Terkel's earlier books, because the respondents speak frequently about the Depression and World War II, the nature of work in America, and what has happened to the American Dream during their lifetimes. In 1997 Terkel published *My American Century*, which collects the best interviews from his previous six works, from *Division Street* through *Coming of Age*. In its own way, however, *Coming of Age* itself does the same thing, if on a lesser scale. Throughout his work Terkel is concerned with certain topics and themes in American life—unions, the effects of the Depression, and the racial divide.

"THE GOOD WAR": AN ORAL HISTORY OF WORLD WAR II (1984). In contrast to other wars, World War II was necessary, Terkel has written elsewhere, because Germany and Japan had to be stopped. Still, as he writes in the introduction to this oral history of World War II, the war was a mixed experience for all its participants: "Food. Fear. Comradeship. And confusion," were some of its basic characteristics. In some ways, in fact, *"The Good War"* seems a continuation of *Hard Times;* in both books the words of the survivors display a sense of camaraderie in untold suffering, triumph after initial defeat. The book was a bestseller and won a Pulitzer Prize for general nonfiction. It is, for some critics, "Terkel's most widely read and in many ways his most powerful and influential book."

The volume includes 120 witnesses to World War II, divided into 4 books over nearly 600 pages. It opens with the testimony of a Hawaiian who was sixteen when the Japanese attacked Pearl Harbor, and then served four long years in the Army, and it ends in the epilogue in the 1980s with kids who do not remember the war but still live under the threat of the atomic bomb. In between are accounts by people who served abroad and at home in the war and in war-related industries, and who talk about the intensity and importance of their experiences.

The subthemes reveal Terkel's awareness of some of the more important issues in American life: African-Americans describe experiences of segregation and discrimination, even when they were involved in the war effort; Japanese Americans describe their incarceration in internment camps on the West Coast and the loss of all they owned. Women describe their experiences in factories, foreshadowing the women's movement that would peak two decades after the war. Critics would complain that Terkel had once again skewed his testimony to support his own social agenda, but supporters would point out that it did not matter. *"The Good War"* gives an accurate testimonial to World War II a decade before films such as *Saving Private Ryan* (1998) and *The Thin Red Line* (1998) were praised for their realism.

The burned and damaged ships USS *West Virginia, Tennessee,* and *Arizona* in Pearl Harbor after the December 7, 1941, attack by the Japanese. *"The Good War": An Oral History of World War II* was an attempt to revisit this tumultuous time, before the generation who lived through it had passed.

RACE: HOW BLACKS AND WHITES THINK AND FEEL ABOUT THE AMERICAN OBSESSION (1992). This collection is perhaps the best example of how Terkel has always tackled the tough topics in American life. In four sections, seventy-eight respondents talk about thirty different subjects: about how race affects friendships, jobs, and education, among other things. *Race* is not a terribly optimistic book, because most of the informants show that prejudice and discrimination have firm holds at every level of American life. There are also stories of courage and hope, as in the prologue of Mamie Mobley, mother of Emmett Till, and the interviews with Lucy Jefferson and Peggy Terry.

Terkel had uncovered this racial divide before—in descriptions of the Japanese American internment camps in *"The Good War,"* for example—but *Race* confronts this issue head on. In fact, the arc of Terkel's career can be seen as the attempt to deal with what he first explored in *Giants of Jazz* and *Division Street:* the schisms such as race that split American society to its roots.

Race does not provide any easy answers, but it helped to initiate a national dialogue and is hopefully part of the healing process. *Race* was later reissued by Terkel's longtime friend and editor, Andre Schiffrin, who had by then left Pantheon to found his own company, The New Press.

Resources

There are no library collections of his work, but the Studs Terkel tape archive—nine thousand hours of interviews, done mostly at WFMT, Chicago—is housed at the Chicago Historical Society, in Chicago, Illinois. Other sources of interest to students of Studs Terkel include the following:

Oral History Associations. Terkel's books are at the center of work in oral history, and those interested in pursuing issues that Terkel raises may wish to find out more about this subject. The Oral History Association, for example, holds annual meetings and since 1973 has sponsored the journal *Oral History Review*. The Oral History Research Center at Indiana University is devoted to "the collection, preservation, and interpretation of memories and oral traditions," particularly in the Midwest. Other regions have their own oral history projects, such as the New England Association of Oral History and the Southwest Oral History Association.

Audio Recordings. Because Terkel spent such a large portion of his career on the radio, there are numerous recordings of his broadcast interviews available. Some of the more accessible recordings include audiocassette versions of his books, *Coming of Age: The Story of Our Century by Those Who've Lived It* (1995), produced by Books on Tape, and *Race: How Blacks and Whites Think and Feel About the American Obsession* (1992), by Brilliance Corporation. In *Telling It Like It Is* (1998), by Alternative Radio, Terkel is interviewed by David Barsamian. Finally, a comprehensive collection called *Voices of Our Time: Five Decades of Studs Terkel Interviews* (1999), released by the HighBridge Company, contains, on five audiocassettes, forty-eight of Terkel's interviews from the 1950s to the 1990s.

Video Recordings. Terkel narrated numerous documentary and educational programs related to American social history, which can be found in libraries. A program based on one of Terkel's own works is *Studs Terkel's "Chicago"* (1985), produced by Home Visions as part of its "Profiles of a Writer" series.

DAVID PECK

Anne Tyler

BORN: October 25, 1941, Minneapolis, Minnesota
IDENTIFICATION: Late-twentieth-century novelist whose books about families have brought her acclaim.

Anne Tyler writes believably about the nature of the family in late twentieth-century America. Her novels demonstrate the difficulty of maintaining communication and connection in today's modern family. Although her fiction could best be called realistic, she balances the often tragic consequences of modern life with delightful, often comic characters, who endure despite catastrophe. Her 1982 *Dinner at the Homesick Restaurant* and her 1985 *The Accidental Tourist* were each nominated for the Pulitzer Prize for fiction. *The Accidental Tourist* won the National Book Critics Circle Award in 1985 and was turned into a movie starring William Hurt, Kathleen Turner, and Geena Davis, who won an Academy Award as best supporting actress. In 1988 *Breathing Lessons* won the Pulitzer Prize in Letters.

The Writer's Life

On October 25, 1941, Anne Phyllis Tyler was born in Minneapolis, Minnesota to Lloyd Parry Tyler, a chemist, and Phyllis Mahon Tyler, a social worker for the Family Welfare Association of Minnesota. She had four younger brothers.

As traditional Quakers, Tyler's parents were particularly interested in creating a home environment that emphasized moral and ethical growth. To that end, the family moved several times in hopes of finding a community that would suit them. Eventually, the Tylers settled in Celo Community, a Quaker commune in Yancy County, North Carolina. There, the Tylers cultivated their own garden, kept goats, and lived in relative isolation. Anne and her brothers were all educated at home until the family moved to Raleigh, North Carolina, in 1952.

Childhood. Tyler's relative isolation at the commune proved beneficial to her writing career. She enjoyed distance from others and developed an objectivity that she used when observing others outside the community. Because her family valued education, Tyler was also exposed to reading and independent study. Her abrupt entry into society when the Tylers moved to Raleigh, however, left her feel-

Raleigh, North Carolina, in the 1950s. The sudden move to the city proved an abrupt shift from the quiet hours of isolation at Tyler's disposal in Celo Community.

ing like an outsider. Consequently, many of Tyler's characters are individuals who feel estranged.

Education. Tyler enrolled in Broughton High School and graduated when she was only sixteen years old. While in high school, she was encouraged in her writing by her teacher Phyllis Peacock. Although Tyler considered attending Swarthmore, she attended Duke University as an Angier B. Duke Scholar. At Duke, Tyler majored in Russian and helped edit *Archive*, a literary magazine. She twice won the Anne Flexner Award for creative writing. Her first short stories, "The Lights on the River," "Laura," "The Bridge," "I Never Saw Morning," and "The Saints in Caesar's Household," were published in *Archive*. In addition, Tyler studied creative writing with Reynolds Price while at Duke.

In 1961, after graduating in three years as a member of Phi Beta Kappa, Tyler went to Columbia University to pursue a master's degree in Russian. She returned to Duke after one year, having completed all requirements for the degree except the thesis. She worked for a time as a bibliographer at the Duke University Library.

Marriage and Early Novels. During this time, Tyler met Taghi Modarressi, an Iranian medical student specializing in child psychiatry. The two married in 1963, then traveled to Iran for a post wedding visit. When they returned to North America, the couple lived in Montreal while Taghi completed his medical residency. Tyler worked at McGill University Law Library while completing her first novel.

Tyler wrote her first two novels, *If Morning Ever Comes* (1964) and *The Tin Can Tree* (1965)

Students stroll the campus of Duke University, date unknown. Duke proved to be another place where Tyler could display her brisk intellect. When the young Russian scholar returned in the role of bibliographer at the university library, she was in charge of ordering books from the Soviet Union.

in Montreal before the birth of her first daughter. These novels earned her some early praise, but not instant success. She did acquire a good friend and editor at Knopf, Judith Jones, who would continue to serve as her editor in the years to come.

After her daughters Tezh and Mitra were born, in 1965 and 1967 respectively, Tyler's writing output slowed as she turned her full attention to motherhood. Her one novel written during this time, "Winter Birds, Winter Apples," has never been published.

Baltimore. In 1967, Tyler and her family moved from Montreal to Baltimore, Maryland, when Taghi received a job offer from the

A view of the Baltimore, Maryland, skyline. The family's move to the port city proved permanent.

University of Maryland Medical School. Once settled in Baltimore, Tyler began to write again. The constraints of caring for two children allowed her to write only stories at first. Although parenthood infringed on her writing time, she believed that it provided deeper and richer life experiences which, in turn, added new dimensions to her work.

After her youngest daughter began nursery school, Tyler started writing even more. She published *A Slipping-Down Life* in 1970 and followed it quickly with *The Clock Winder* in 1972. Both novels show new levels of emotional and literary sophistication. In 1972 Tyler also began writing book reviews for the *National Observer*. After this initial publication, her book-reviewing skills were showcased in many journals and newspapers, including *The New York Times Book Review*.

Favorable Reviews, Then Disappointment.

Tyler's next four novels began to receive more favorable attention, and as a result she received several prestigious awards. Novelist Gail Godwin enthusiastically reviewed *Celestial Navigation* (1974) in *The New York Times Book Review*, and John Updike gave a positive evaluation of *Searching for Caleb* (1976) in *The New Yorker*. These reviews by established authors and critics helped to establish Tyler's reputation in the literary market. In 1977 Tyler received a citation of merit from the American Academy and Institute of Arts and Letters.

Although critics believed Tyler was due for a breakthrough commercial success, it eluded her. During the late 1970's, her family felt many pressures related to the Iranian revolution because of her husband's nationality. These pressures may have been partially responsible for Tyler's problems with her next novel, "Pantaleo," which she decided should not be published. Even her quirky *Morgan's Passing* (1980) received little critical attention.

The Turning Point. With the 1982 publication of *Dinner at the Homesick Restaurant*, Tyler finally achieved critical acclaim as well as commercial success. This novel was nominated for a Pulitzer Prize, and the same year, Tyler won the PEN/Faulkner Award for Fiction. In addition to this much-deserved success, *The Accidental Tourist*, published in 1985, earned Tyler even more public favor. This novel was also nominated for a Pulitzer Prize and won the National Book Critics Circle Award before being made into a 1988 film starring William Hurt, Kathleen Turner, and Geena Davis. Davis won the Best Supporting Actress Award for her portrayal of Muriel Pritchett.

After the Pulitzer. Although Tyler's next novel, *Breathing Lessons*, won a Pulitzer Prize in 1988, many critics saw it as a step down from *The Accidental Tourist*. Her novels after *Breathing Lessons*, though still distinctly Anne Tyler novels, did not receive as many awards as the works from her middle period. Her novels of the 1990's—*Saint Maybe* (1991), *Ladder of Years* (1995), and *A Patchwork Planet* (1998)—each lacked the critical and commercial success of Tyler's middle-period fiction.

In addition to her novels and short stories, Tyler wrote *Tumble Tower* (1993), a children's book that her daughter Mitra illustrated. After Tyler's husband, Taghi, died in 1997, she dedicated *A Patchwork Planet* to him. A very private person, Tyler was rarely known to leave the Baltimore home where she continued to write.

FILMS BASED ON TYLER'S STORIES

1988 *The Accidental Tourist*

1994 *Breathing Lessons* (TV)

1998 *Saint Maybe* (TV)

1999 *Earthly Possessions* (TV)

1999 *A Slipping-Down Life*

A reclusive, solitary figure, Tyler is seen here sharing a tender moment with the family pet in 1991.

HIGHLIGHTS IN TYLER'S LIFE

1941	Anne Phyllis Tyler is born on October 25 in Minneapolis, Minnesota.
1948	Family moves to Celo Community, a Quaker commune, in the mountains of North Carolina.
1952	Family moves to Raleigh, North Carolina; Tyler attends Broughton High School.
1958	Tyler enrolls in Duke University; majors in Russian; publishes first short stories in campus literary magazine, *Archive*.
1961	Graduates from Duke with a bachelor's degree in Russian.
1961–1962	Pursues a master's degree in Russian at Columbia, but returns to North Carolina without finishing thesis.
1963	Marries Taghi Modarressi, an Iranian medical student; moves to Montreal while Modarressi completes his residency.
1964	Publishes first novel, *If Morning Ever Comes*; begins long friendship with Knopf editor Judith Jones.
1965	Publishes *The Tin Can Tree*; first daughter, Tezh, is born.
1967	Second daughter, Mitra, is born; family moves to Baltimore.
1972	Publishes first book review in the *National Observer*.
1977	Receives citation of merit from the American Academy and Institute of Arts and Letters.
1980	Is awarded the Janet Heidinger Kafka Prize.
1982	Publishes *Dinner at the Homesick Restaurant*; wins PEN/Faulkner Award for Fiction.
1983	Is elected a member of the American Academy and Institute of Arts and Letters.
1985	*The Accidental Tourist* wins National Book Critics Circle Award for Fiction.
1988	*Breathing Lessons* receives the Pulitzer Prize for fiction.
1993	Publishes children's book, *Tumble Tower*, with illustrations by daughter Mitra Modarressi.
1997	Husband, Taghi Modarressi, dies.
1998	Tyler publishes *A Patchwork Planet*.

THE *NEW YORK TIMES* BESTSELLER

WINNER OF THE PULITZER PRIZE

Anne Tyler

AUTHOR OF *LADDER OF YEARS*

BREATHING LESSONS

"More powerful and moving than anything she has done."—*Los Angeles Times*

The Writer's Work

Anne Tyler has written long and short fiction, as well as a children's book and many book reviews. She is, however, best known for her long fiction. Although Tyler's fiction is praised by critics for its sharp attention to detail, charming characters, and effective dialogue, it is also characterized by a realistic, yet tragicomic, vision of families in the modern world.

Themes in Tyler's Fiction. Tyler frequently explores in her fiction the desire of an individ-

D. K. Mocialskij's *Quattro Generazioni* (*Four Generations*) captures the tenderness and warmth Tyler draws from her elaborate analysis of families. According to critic Edward Hoagland, her work is marked by "zest and an appetite for whatever, just as long as families stay together. She wants her characters plausibly married and caring for each other."

ual to belong to a family group, as well as the restrictions that such belonging engenders. Although she most often presents the positive side of family structures, she never sentimentalizes family life. Indeed, some families, such as the Emersons of *The Clock Winder*, appear to be fragmented and dysfunctional, even cold-hearted. Others, such as the Learys in *The Accidental Tourist*, are so tightly knit that members cannot leave. In both kinds of families, individuals feel restricted and often unloved. Some, such as Charlotte Emory in *Earthly Possessions* and Delia Grinstead in *Ladder of Years*, simply leave.

Tyler characters who do flee typically return to their families, or they form new families. Either outcome indicates the endurance of the group, and the individual as well. This theme of endurance runs throughout Tyler's works and accounts for much of the positive nature of her vision.

People in Tyler's Fiction. Tyler's early characters are usually ordinary, middle-class people living in North Carolina. In later novels, almost all the characters live in Baltimore. In both her novels and short stories, Tyler showcases one family and its particular struggles to overcome its limitations. Her characters, while often trapped in mundane existences, are richly drawn and often display endearingly quirky characteristics. Morgan Gower in *Morgan's Passing*, for example, likes to dress in costume and pretend to be someone different; Charlotte

Tyler's characters struggle to find a clearly defined role amidst their often tumultuous and ever-shifting family life. As in Diana Ong's painting *Crowd XX*, there is sometimes a vague boundary between where the individual stops and the group begins.

Emory's father in *Earthly Possessions* has a photo studio where he dresses clients in exotic costumes that best represent their true selves.

This tendency of Tyler's characters to re-create themselves as a method of enduring underscores her abiding faith in art and the artist's ability to create something new. In most of Tyler's major novels, artists use their crafts as a way to impose some order on their worlds. In some novels, such as *Celestial Navigation*, the struggle between being an artist and being part of a family is the central conflict. Tyler's characters have many different artistic outlets—photography, sculpting, costuming, puppeteering, writing, and even

SOME INSPIRATIONS BEHIND TYLER'S WORK

Although Anne Tyler was born in Minnesota, her family moved to a Quaker commune known as Celo Community in rural North Carolina in 1948, when Tyler was seven years old. Tyler's relative isolation at this commune led to her earliest moments of imagining herself as other people, one of the initial impulses that later spurred her to write fiction. When Tyler moved to Raleigh in 1952, her sense of being an outsider there also informed many of her later characters' same concerns. In her early years, Tyler also greatly valued instruction from her Broughton High School writing teacher, Phyllis Peacock, as well as from her creative writing teacher at Duke University, Reynolds Price.

Critics have noted many influences in her writing, including those of Ralph Waldo Emerson, William Faulkner, and Anton Chekhov, but none is as important as Eudora Welty. Tyler frequently stated that reading Welty taught her the value of detail, as well as the value of writing a story or novel about an ordinary, but well-examined, subject. Tyler, like Welty, understands and appreciates character, as well as place.

Tyler, more so than many of her contemporaries, has shown the importance of place in fiction. Although three of her early novels are set in North Carolina, the bulk of her fiction is set in and around Baltimore, Maryland. Her use of Baltimore culture and the names of actual places there help to create the sense that all of Tyler's fiction inhabits one large canvas.

Being cloistered in the rustic backcountry of Mount Celo, North Carolina, proved fortuitous to the budding novelist. It sparked her imagination and compelled her to create alternate personas.

Diana Ong's painting *Destiny 1* suggests the dislocation and search for identity that often underpins Tyler's work. People seem to be a unit when in truth the backdrop of the family makes their individual loneliness all the more pronounced.

frame-making—and each helps establish that character in the particular novel.

A Tragicomic Vision. Many of Tyler's works contain tragic elements that threaten to destroy individuals as well as family structures. In *The Accidental Tourist*, Macon Leary's only son

Ethan is shot in a fast-food restaurant. His son's death destroys Macon's marriage and threatens to destroy his sanity. In *The Clock Winder*, Timothy Emerson commits suicide after cheating on a medical school exam; his tragic death drives Elizabeth Abbott out of the family.

Despite undercurrents of tragedy, Tyler manages to include sufficient amounts of comedy in order to prevent characters from being consumed by their difficulties. In *The Accidental Tourist*, Macon Leary is rescued, in part, because of Muriel Pritchett, whose inappropriate behavior and antics lighten Macon's despair and offset the tragedy in the novel. This pairing of tragic and comic characters and events helps keep Tyler's novels off-center, allowing them to maintain their seriousness without sacrificing their humor.

Tyler's Literary Legacy. It is too early to gauge what impact Tyler's novels and short stories might have on American literature. Her work has been characterized by critics as domestic fiction or novels of manners—both descriptions limiting her work to the small, circumscribed area of the household. However, Tyler may best be remembered for her accuracy in tackling the more universal issue of the family and its importance to the individual.

Although Tyler's novels of the 1980's, such as *The Accidental Tourist* and *Breathing Lessons*, sold well and attracted great critical attention, her later works did not have the same impact. Tyler's work has always appealed to general readers, perhaps more so than to literary scholars. Many of her short stories have appeared in magazines as diverse as *Ladies' Home Journal* and *The New Yorker*.

Despite her slight decrease in popularity in the 1990's, Tyler remains one of the foremost chroniclers of the family in transition. Her novels portray the shifting configuration of the family as it evolves from the nuclear to the more fragmented variations found in American culture at the end of the twentieth century.

BIBLIOGRAPHY

Bennett, Barbara A. "Attempting to Connect: Verbal Humor in the Novels of Anne Tyler." *South Atlantic Review* 60 (1995): 57–75.

Carson, Barbara Harrell. "Complicate, Complicate: Anne Tyler's Moral Imperative." *Southern Quarterly* 31 (Fall 1992): 24–34.

Croft, Robert W. *Anne Tyler: A Bio-Bibliography.* Westport, Conn.: Greenwood Press, 1995.

_____. *An Anne Tyler Companion.* Westport, Conn.: Greenwood Press, 1998.

Evans, Elizabeth. *Anne Tyler.* New York: Twayne Publishers, 1993.

Petry, Alice Hall. *Understanding Anne Tyler.* Columbia: University of South Carolina Press, 1990.

____, ed. *Critical Essays on Anne Tyler.* New York: G. K. Hall, 1992.

Salwak, Dale, ed. *Anne Tyler as Novelist.* Iowa City: University of Iowa Press, 1994.

Stephens, C. Ralph, ed. *The Fiction of Anne Tyler.* Jackson: University Press of Mississippi, 1990.

Sweeney, Susan Elizabeth. "Anne Tyler's Invented Games: *The Accidental Tourist* and *Breathing Lessons.*" *Southern Quarterly* 34 (1995): 81–97.

Voelker, Joseph C. *Art and the Accidental in Anne Tyler.* Columbia: University of Missouri Press, 1989.

LONG FICTION

1964   If Morning Ever Comes
1965   The Tin Can Tree
1970   A Slipping-Down Life
1972   The Clock Winder
1974   Celestial Navigation
1976   Searching for Caleb
1977   Earthly Possessions
1980   Morgan's Passing
1982   Dinner at the Homesick Restaurant
1985   The Accidental Tourist
1988   Breathing Lessons
1991   Saint Maybe
1995   Ladder of Years
1998   A Patchwork Planet

CHILDREN'S LITERATURE

1993   Tumble Tower

THE #1 NEW YORK TIMES BESTSELLER BY THE PULITZER PRIZE–WINNING AUTHOR OF *LADDER OF YEARS*

Anne Tyler

The ACCIDENTAL TOURIST

THE ACCIDENTAL TOURIST

Genre: Novel
Subgenre: Tragicomic realism
Published: New York, 1985
Time period: 1980s
Setting: Baltimore, Maryland

Themes and Issues. The title of *The Accidental Tourist* conveys many of its themes. Macon Leary, the main character of the novel, does not like to travel or venture outside his safe, self-constructed world. When he travels—either literally or figuratively—he prefers to have certain rituals in place to make these trips safe. Yet Macon must learn to become a tourist in all senses of the word, learning more about others and himself in the process. This novel, more than most of Tyler's novels, also combines the extremes of tragedy and comedy to convey its message.

The Plot. Macon Leary writes travel books for businessmen who do not want to leave home or experience anything odd or unusual. The idea for his travel books arose from his own fear of being around "outsiders," or anyone who is not a member of his immediate family. Although he does marry and have a child, Ethan, Macon never really loses his need for his birth family. After his son's death in a freak shooting at a fast-food restaurant, Macon must come to terms with his fears. He leaves his wife and moves back home with his two brothers and his sister Rose.

The early parts of the novel concern Macon's coping with both the loss of his son and the fragmentation of his marriage. His dog, Edward, requires immediate attention. Like that of his master, Edward's personality has altered; they both need to be "tamed." Macon takes Edward to a kennel. There he meets the very unusual Muriel Pritchett, who tames Edward and melts Macon's reserve.

Entirely wrong for Macon, Muriel is a single mother living on a small income; her language and appearance show her to be somewhat beneath the Learys' level of economic and cultural status. Unlike other women, however, Muriel starts to pull Macon out of his depression. Her son Alexander, an asthmatic, also appeals to Macon. Toward the end of the novel, Macon threatens to return to his wife, but an impromptu trip to France with Muriel ends up providing the right environment for Macon to commit to Muriel and her son. The Pritchetts are people who need him, and as a consequence of being needed, Macon learns to overcome the trauma of his son's death.

Analysis. This story illustrates both the problems and the privileges of the nuclear family. Although Tyler paints the Learys as particularly unusual, they all have common rituals that give order to their lives and provide a framework for their family structure. Their unusual character traits provide much of the humor of the novel. The brothers and sister, for example, play an elaborate card game known as Vaccination, which outsiders can never learn to play because they are unable to understand the game's constantly changing rules.

Macon Leary, the protagonist of the story, suffers from the family's stagnation, but by the time he leaves to develop a new life with the unlikely Muriel Pritchett, his boss finds happiness within the very structure that Macon has to leave. By viewing the family from these two different perspectives, Tyler conveys the conflicting feelings of familial comfort and familial restriction.

SOURCES FOR FURTHER STUDY

Croft, Robert W. *An Anne Tyler Companion*. Westport, Conn.: Greenwood Press, 1998.

Humphrey, Lin T. "Exploration of a Not-So-Accidental Novel." In *Anne Tyler as Novelist*, edited by Dale Salwak. Iowa City: University of Iowa Press, 1994.

Petry, Alice Hall. *Understanding Anne Tyler*. Columbia: University of South Carolina Press, 1990.

Donald Martin's *Portrait (In Middle Age)* presents a portrait of a disjointed, incomplete man. In *The Accidental Tourist*, Macon realizes he must change if he is ever to find wholeness in his life again. While staring at an old family portrait one evening, he suddenly notices his brothers and sister were still "sitting in much the same positions. . . . Was there any real change? He felt a jolt of something very close to panic. Here he still was! The same as ever! What have I gone and done? He wondered, and he swallowed thickly and looked at his own empty hands."

BREATHING LESSONS

Genre: Novel
Subgenre: Domestic realism
Published: New York, 1988
Time period: 1980s
Setting: Baltimore, Maryland

Themes and Issues. Tyler's novel *Breathing Lessons* tackles the complicated problems that occur when a woman tries too hard to make her family ideal. Although Maggie Moran is sincere in her wish to bring her son and estranged daughter-in-law back together, she risks complete alienation from her family as she attempts to manipulate everyone in it, including her husband, Ira; her granddaughter, Leroy; her son, Jesse; and her daughter-in-law, Fiona. The novel explores Maggie's use of manipulative language and gestures to achieve her goals, as well as her husband Ira's equally manipulative silences. Tyler focuses the novel on the inherent dangers of communication breakdowns within the family.

The Plot. Maggie and Ira Moran hear of their childhood friend's death and decide to travel to his funeral in a neighboring city. The trip becomes an opportunity for Maggie and Ira to explore elements of their past with their old friends and also allows for Maggie to see

In *Breathing Lessons*, Maggie is the victim of sentimentalized notions of family, such as the one depicted in Joseph Clark's *The Flower of the Flock*. She is forced to acknowledge that her ideal is just that, a construction, a fantasy image hardly fulfilled by the flawed and very real family in which she lives.

her estranged daughter-in-law and granddaughter.

Maggie, unbeknownst to anyone, has visited and even spied on her granddaughter before this day, but on the day of the trip, she convinces Ira to stop at her former daughter-in-law's home for a visit. At this meeting, Maggie convinces Fiona to return to Baltimore with them by telling Fiona that she believes her son to still be in love with her. Because Fiona sentimentally hopes for Jesse's love, she trusts Maggie's words and returns with the family to Baltimore.

Unfortunately, Maggie has misrepresented her son to Fiona. Maggie believes that the two need only to see each other to get back together, but she completely ignores the fact that Jesse is too immature to accept responsibility for his daughter, Leroy. No longer interested in Fiona at all, Jesse is already dating another woman. When the two meet at the end of the novel, Fiona quickly realizes that Maggie has not been truthful. When Ira suddenly tells Fiona of Jesse's newest girlfriend, Fiona leaves with Leroy. As a consequence, Maggie must come to terms with her own meddling and its impact on others, including her husband. She is forced to consider how her manipulations have affected her relationship with Ira.

Analysis. Although *Breathing Lessons* won the 1998 Pulitzer Prize for fiction, many critics view it merely as Tyler's quintessential domestic novel, a designation that often carries negative connotations. Because Maggie is the protagonist of the story, the reader becomes immersed in the small details of her life, as well as her lies and manipulations. In this respect, the limited vision of the character takes on a domestic sensibility. However, the novel is more than just an exploration of the humdrum details of a household and its members. *Breathing Lessons* examines the importance of communicating honestly and appropriately in order to build and maintain relationships. Fulfilling one of Tyler's recurring themes, Maggie's relationship with her husband endures despite her unconscionable meddling.

SOURCES FOR FURTHER STUDY

Croft, Robert W. *An Anne Tyler Companion.* Westport, Conn.: Greenwood Press, 1998.

Sweeney, Susan Elizabeth. "Anne Tyler's Invented Games: *The Accidental Tourist* and *Breathing Lessons.*" *Southern Quarterly* 34 (1995): 81–97.

Wagner-Martin, Linda. "*Breathing Lessons*: A Domestic Success Story." In *Anne Tyler as Novelist*, edited by Dale Salwak. Iowa City: University of Iowa Press, 1994.

DINNER AT THE HOMESICK RESTAURANT
Genre: Novel
Subgenre: Tragicomic realism
Published: New York, 1982
Time period: 1970s
Setting: Baltimore, Maryland

Themes and Issues. Like many of Tyler's novels, *Dinner at the Homesick Restaurant* explores the individuals' struggles within the confinement of their families. The main characters, all children of Pearl and Beck Tull, try to run from their family, even as they find themselves inexplicably drawn back to try making it work. Unlike many of Tyler's novels, however, *Dinner at the Homesick Restaurant* traces the family's history to underscore the mother and absent father's influence on their three children. The Tulls endure in spite of their problems, underscoring Tyler's preoccupation with the abiding strength of the nuclear family.

The Plot. *Dinner at the Homesick Restaurant* is told through a series of flashbacks from Pearl Tull's deathbed. Pearl relates the events that led up to her marriage to Beck Tull, a traveling salesman, as well as the subsequent birth of her three children—Ezra, Cody, and Jenny. When the children are relatively young, Beck leaves on one of his sales trips and never returns. Pearl is unwilling to tell the children of her inability to keep her husband, and she goes to work and continues to pretend that Beck will someday return.

Pearl's constant fear that she will be unable to provide for her children leads her to work too hard to maintain their physical needs, and

In Dale Kennington's *Caffe Florian*, the patrons seem to occupy their own separate worlds. In *Dinner at the Homesick Restaurant*, Pearl Tull's children are similarly isolated by the way she raised them. Each has radically different views of their mother. She is alternately abusive, suspicious, and nurturing.

too little to maintain their emotional needs. All of the children ultimately suffer because of her inability to provide them with emotional sustenance. Ezra withdraws and becomes an underachiever, sure that his only goal in life is to provide nourishment to others. Toward that end, he takes over a restaurant, the aptly titled Homesick Restaurant of the book's title, and prepares only the eclectic foods that he thinks his visitors "need." His goal for most of the novel is to bring his family together for one meal at his restaurant.

Cody, Pearl's second son, suffers from the need to be loved. Feeling that Ezra has always been firstborn, first loved, Cody intentionally sabotages all of Ezra's endeavors; most notably, he steals Ezra's one true love, Ruth, away from him. Although Cody is the most financially successful of the three siblings, he constantly doubts himself because of his inability to feel at home in his environment. Deprived of emotional "food," Cody knows very little about how to give or receive love; his life is a series of business successes and relationship failures.

His only son runs away from home at the end of the novel, because Cody is unable to show him love.

Jenny Tull, the youngest child and only daughter, also feels the emotional vacuum within her family. She has been crippled by two unhappy marriages and feels compelled to take on more than she can emotionally endure in her search to find a "family." By the end of the novel, she finds happiness as a pediatric doctor and the new stepmother of six "abandoned" children.

The novel ends after another botched meal at Ezra's restaurant, this one following Pearl Tull's funeral. Ironically, Beck Tull, the absent parent, shows up for this meal that threatens to end in verbal meltdown. Despite the family's historic lack of support for each other, the almost-completed meal suggests that the family has stayed together because they have continually tried, however ineptly, to make it work.

Analysis. *Dinner at the Homesick Restaurant* sharply displays a family fractured by divorce and emotional sterility. As in many of Tyler's novels, the children must pay the price for the family's fragmentation and dysfunction. In many ways, the novel hints at how family members need to emotionally respond to each other.

When the novel was published in 1982, critics hailed it as Tyler's breakthrough work. It eventually would be nominated for the National Book Award and would prove to be her first major success with a public audience as well. Although it is bleaker than some of her other works, *Dinner at the Homesick Restaurant* remains one of Tyler's most influential and critically acclaimed novels.

SOURCES FOR FURTHER STUDY

Eckard, Paula Gallant. "Family and Community in Anne Tyler's *Dinner at the Homesick Restaurant.*" *Southern Literary Journal* 10 (Spring 1990): 33–44.

Town, Caren. "Rewriting the Family During *Dinner at the Homesick Restaurant.*" *Southern Quarterly* 31 (Fall 1992): 14–23.

Wagner, Joseph B. "Beck Tull: 'The Absent Presence' in *Dinner at the Homesick Restaurant.*" In *The Fiction of Anne Tyler*, edited by C. Ralph Stephens. Jackson: University Press of Mississippi, 1990.

Other Works

CELESTIAL NAVIGATION (1974). One of Anne Tyler's most autobiographical novels, *Celestial Navigation* concerns the emotional growth of Jeremy Pauling, a middle-aged agoraphobic artist whose life is dramatically changed when his mother dies and leaves him to fend for himself. When Jeremy's sisters arrive to tie up the loose ends of their mother's death, they find that Jeremy is ill-suited to care for himself. He lives in his own home but is surrounded by boarders that he and his mother have taken in to support themselves financially. Jeremy knows how to do little except make sculptures from things found in his home.

When Mary Tell escapes her husband and arrives at Jeremy's boardinghouse with her daughter Darcy, a romance between the two seems unlikely. Yet, Mary and Jeremy enter into an arrangement that seems to be fruitful for both of them: Jeremy gains a companion and a family to support him and his artistic endeavors, and Mary feels comfort and love with Jeremy, Darcy, and the many children and other boarders who live around them.

Jeremy's inability to leave the house, however, creates the central conflict in the novel. Although they essentially live together as husband and wife for many years, Mary and Jeremy can only legally marry once her divorce becomes final. At that point, Mary believes that Jeremy should be able to venture out with her to be married. Jeremy, however, loses his ability to cope with the outside world and cannot go through with the wedding. As a consequence, Mary and her family leave home to live in a fishing shack owned by Jeremy's art dealer, Brian. In his most noble act, Jeremy braves the outside world to try and win Mary back, but when the two meet outside the confines of the home, the relationship seems doomed to failure. Mary and the children do not return home and Jeremy seems destined to live a sadder and more diminished life without Mary.

Tyler has said that Jeremy Pauling is the character in her fiction who most closely resembles her own sense of self. Tyler's use of a boardinghouse family underscores her belief in the importance of familial structure, and the value of the nuclear family in maintaining connection and providing growth, even if the family is constructed from the spare members of other families.

EARTHLY POSSESSIONS (1977).

Told from the perspective of thirty-five-year-old Charlotte Emory, *Earthly Possessions* chronicles her being kidnapped by demolition derby driver Jake Simms, as the two travel to Florida to pick up his pregnant girlfriend Mindy from a home for wayward girls. Ironically, Charlotte's kidnapping occurs on the day she has decided to leave her husband and the group of family members and church members that is living at her home. During her trip with Jake, Charlotte gradually begins to open up to Jake, and he learns her reasons for wanting to leave.

The only daughter of a grotesquely fat woman and a thin, retiring photographer, Charlotte has spent her entire life feeling as if she did not belong in her own family. Indeed, she often felt she had been switched at birth and dreamed of belonging to that other family. She eventually marries Saul Emory, the boy next door, who soon decides to attend Bible college and become a minister. As a result, Charlotte's home becomes a way station for all who need a place to go. She adopts children, old people, and any stray who needs somewhere to live. All of Saul's brothers come back to stay with them. Charlotte feels saddled with responsibility and as a result, eventually desires to flee.

During the course of their travels, the two become friends and Charlotte ends up helping Jake rather than falling victim to him. Ironically, Jake Simms's more complicated and pathetic life forces Charlotte out of her desire to travel and get away from her own life. After Charlotte helps Jake and Mindy resolve their problems and returns home to Saul, she finds a deeper sense of her place within her family. As a result of her travels and her discussions with Jake, she discovers that she can change and travel in the future without actually having to leave her home. She realizes that change is inevitable regardless of where she lives.

A PATCHWORK PLANET (1998).

Barnaby Gaitlin belongs to a good Baltimore family, but he has done very little with his life. In fact, he has become the black sheep of the family because he once broke into other people's homes. Partially as a result of this incident, he is estranged from his family. He rents a basement apartment and works as an assistant for Rent-a-Back, a service for those who are unable to do physical tasks.

Although Gaitlin's work seems noble in some ways, his life consists of putting up Christmas trees or buying groceries for the elderly and the infirm. His ex-wife, Natalie, is remarried to a prosperous businessman, and whenever he visits his daughter Opal he gets the distinct sensation that Opal is pulling away from him in favor of her new family. In addition, Barnaby's father and brother both work at the family business; the guardians of the family's extensive trust fund, they feel that Barnaby is merely wasting his life. At home, Barnaby can do nothing right except in the eyes of his mother's more middle-class parents.

Through a series of misadventures, Barnaby meets Sophia Maynard, who works at a bank and seems to be a model citizen. He believes that she is both literally and figuratively an angel, in fulfillment of the family myth that each male has at some time been visited by an angel who tells him what he is supposed to do with his life. He sees Sophia as his destiny and begins to date her. Things seem to go well until

In John S. Bunker's 1997 *Springtime Angel*, a woman appears half mortal, half divine. The family myth that an angel visits the men of the Gaitlin family to supply them with their destiny proves to be a misleading and destructive illusion in Tyler's novel *A Patchwork Planet*. For Barnaby, the angel comes in the guise he least suspects.

Barnaby is suspected of stealing a large sum of money from Sophia's aunt's flour bin. Sophia, believing him guilty, takes her own money and places it in the flour bin. This lack of trust in him alters Barnaby's perception of Sophia, and the relationship breaks down.

Ironically, Martine, a lower-class woman who works with Barnaby, sees him for his best self. She does not expect Barnaby to have a grand career, but she knows perfectly well that he can be trusted. As a result, Barnaby finds his angel in a very unexpected place, but in time for him to find some happiness in spite of his family's rejection.

SEARCHING FOR CALEB (1976).

This novel spans the rather lengthy history of the Pecks, an old, established Baltimore family. Two sons, Daniel and Caleb Peck, are born to Justin Peck in the late nineteenth century. Although both boys are born into a prosperous family, each takes a different avenue in life.

Daniel has a rather conventional existence, even though he is deserted by his wife, Margaret Rose, and has to raise his five children alone. He becomes a lawyer and remains upright and conservative his entire life. His brother Caleb, however, runs away from home as a young man and is never heard from again. At the novel's opening in 1972, Daniel, now ninety-two, is in search of his long-lost brother with the help of his granddaughter, Justine.

Justine Peck, a fortune-teller and drifter herself, has married a first cousin, Duncan Peck, and the two lead a sort of gypsy lifestyle, traveling around Baltimore while Justine tells fortunes and Duncan takes up part-time work. Duncan, like the earlier Caleb, gets restless and leaves jobs. Consequently, the family picks up and leaves its home every few months. Duncan and Justine have a daughter, Meg, who is the opposite of her immediate family; she constantly strives to maintain order and a sense of permanence.

The plot centers on Justine's search for the missing Caleb, whom she eventually finds in Louisiana, where he has been living and playing blues harmonica since escaping from Baltimore many years ago. She brings him back to see his long-lost brother, but before the two can meet, Caleb slips away once more. At the end of the novel, Daniel Peck dies, and the reunion that has been sought after for so long effectively dies with him.

Justine, however, frustrated with her husband's inability to keep a job and her daughter's rejection of their lifestyle, eventually finds the solution that will make her the happiest—she finds work for Duncan as a mechanic for a traveling circus so he can move around but still keep working. The novel ends with the youngest Pecks being able to resolve their differences in temperament, something that Caleb and Daniel could not do.

Resources

The major collection of Anne Tyler's papers can be found at the Perkins Library at Duke University. It includes her personal correspondence, reviews of her work, promotional materials, and periodicals in which her works appeared. In addition, the collection includes copies of her books in all editions, as well as manuscript versions of her novels. Other sources of interest to students of Anne Tyler include the following:

Featured Author: Anne Tyler. *The New York Times* on the World Wide Web hosts the most extensive online collection of Tyler materials, including reviews of her books, articles about Tyler, an interview, and essays and book reviews she has written. (http://www.nytimes.com/books/98/04/19/specials/tyler.html)

Audiobooks. Many of Anne Tyler's later novels are available in unabridged recordings from Books On Tape and Recorded Books, Inc. Recorded titles include *A Patchwork Planet* (1998), *Ladder of Years* (1995), *Saint Maybe* (1991), and *The Accidental Tourist* (1986).

REBECCA HENDRICK FLANNAGAN

Alice Walker

BORN: February 9, 1944, Eatonton, Georgia
IDENTIFICATION: Modern African American fiction writer, poet, essayist, editor, and activist whose popular womanist works engage readers and inspire them to confront issues of violence and oppression in society.

Alice Walker is perhaps the most significant African American woman writer of the post-1960s era. She strongly advocates, through her writing and activities, a global brand of "womanism," crusading against the oppression of racism and sexism. She is best known for her novel *The Color Purple* (1982), which became a best-seller, won a Pulitzer Prize, and was filmed under the direction of Steven Spielberg (1985). The controversial story of African American women oppressed both by a racist society and by the men of their own race included plot elements of rape, incest, and lesbianism. In Walker's essays and articles, poems, short stories, and novels, which are widely read and often taught, she alerts her readers to the need for change in the treatment of black women both in the United States and in Africa.

On February 9, 1944, Alice Malsenior Walker was born in a small cabin in Eatonton, Georgia. She was the youngest of eight children born to Willie Lee Walker, a tenant farmer, and Minnie Tallulah Grant Walker, who helped her husband in the fields and also worked as a maid. Walker enjoyed hearing the stories both her parents told. However, it was her mother who most strongly influenced her. Minnie's devotion to her flower garden taught Walker to love beauty; Minnie's insistence that her children stay in school, even when the white landlord urged her to have them quit, taught Walker the value of education.

Childhood. Despite her family's poverty, Walker's early years were relatively happy. She enjoyed playing outdoors with her older brothers and she also liked to get dressed up and look her prettiest. However, when she was eight, she was hit in the right eye by a shot from her brother's BB gun. She lost her sight in that eye and was also badly scarred. Believing that she was ugly, Walker withdrew into herself, becoming an observer of life rather than a participant in it. Ironically, she later said that this period of isolation was what made her into a writer. Encouraged by her mother, Walker read voraciously and also started writing poems. She had an operation when she was fourteen that eliminated her scars and partially restored her vision. She went on to become both senior class queen and valedictorian at her high school; her future had been decided.

This rural home in southeastern Georgia reflects the modest cabin in which Walker was born in 1944.

Into the World. Walker's injury qualified her for a scholarship to Spelman College, and in 1961, with seventy-five dollars that her neighbors in Eatonton had raised for her bus fare, she departed for Atlanta, Georgia. There she soon became active in the Civil Rights movement. However, because the college administration discouraged its faculty and students from becoming involved in those activities, Walker decided to accept a scholarship offered her by Sarah Lawrence College in Bronxville, New York, which was much more liberal in its policies.

In the summer of 1964 Walker traveled in Africa. When she returned home in the fall, she had to deal with the fact that she was pregnant. Well aware of her father's disapproval of out-of-wedlock childbirth and her mother's horror of abortion, she seriously considered suicide. However, she did have an abortion. In the days that followed, she turned out one poem after another, passing them on to the poet Muriel Rukeyser, who was one of her teachers. Rukeyser was impressed by the poems and took steps to get them accepted for publication. These poems constitute most of those in *Once: Poems*, which appeared in 1968.

Walker received her bachelor's degree from Sarah Lawrence in the spring of 1965. She spent that summer canvassing voters in Liberty County, Georgia. In the fall, she moved to New York City, where she worked in the daytime and wrote at night.

Mississippi, Marriage, and Motherhood. Determined to take a more active part in the Civil Rights movement, in the summer of 1966

Walker (third from left, seated on arm of chair) is seen here with her fellow students at Spelman College in Atlanta, Georgia, in the early 1960s. Strongly opposed to political activism, Spelman sought to graduate "proper" young women. Never one to allow herself to be restricted, Walker enrolled at the liberal and prestigious Sarah Lawrence College in Bronxville, New York, in 1963.

This photograph of Walker was taken in New York City's Central Park on August 12, 1970, while the up-and-coming writer was being interviewed about her first novel, *The Third Life of Grange Copeland*.

Wellesley, Massachusetts, and at the University of Massachusetts-Boston.

Death and Decisions. In 1973 Walker's father, Willie Lee Walker, died, leaving the memory of an embittered man whom age had only made more violent. That year Walker published two more books: her first collection of short stories, *In Love and Trouble: Stories of Black Women*, and her second volume of poetry, *Revolutionary Petunias*.

In 1974 Melvyn Leventhal and Alice Walker moved back to New York City. Walker became a contributing editor for *Ms.* magazine; finished her novel *Meridian* (1976); wrote more poems, short stories, and a biography for children, *Langston Hughes: American Poet*; and worked on an anthology of the works of Zora Neale Hurston, a writer of the 1920s Harlem Renaissance whom Walker had discovered while living in Mississippi. In Hurston, Walker found a kindred spirit, and in Hurston's way of retelling old stories in order to preserve the cultural heritage, she found a pattern and a purpose for her own work.

Meanwhile, Walker was making some momentous decisions about her life. In 1976 she and Leventhal were divorced. Two years later, she moved to San Francisco, California. In 1979 Walker published a third volume of poems and the impressive volume entitled *I Love Myself When I Am Laughing . . . and Then Again When I Am Looking Mean and Impressive: A Zora Neale Hurston Reader*. The next year, she received a prestigious Guggenheim Fellowship. However, it was her third novel that made Walker both famous and financially secure.

Walker abandoned her plans for a stay in Senegal in western Africa and instead moved to Mississippi. There she met Melvyn Rosenman Leventhal, a Jewish civil rights attorney. After a year in New York City, they were married and returned to Mississippi, settling in Jackson, where they remained for seven years. In 1969 their daughter, Rebecca Grant, was born. Three days earlier, Walker had finished her first novel, *The Third Life of Grange Copeland* (1970).

While she was in Mississippi, Walker taught at both Jackson State College and Tougeloo College. She also spent eighteen months in the North, teaching at Wellesley College in

Fame, Fortune, and Film. Walker's third novel, *The Color Purple*, was both a critical and a popular success. It was admired by critics, won an American Book Award and a Pulitzer Prize, and stayed on the *New York Times* bestseller list for twenty-five weeks. The movie rights were sold to Warner Brothers for $350,000.

The film *The Color Purple* was directed by Steven Spielberg. It, too, was extremely popular. With her earnings from the book and the film, Walker was at last financially secure. Moreover, even though she was understandably upset about the ongoing attacks on her work and her motives for writing the novel, it was gratifying to see that both the book and the film were widely assigned to students in history and literature classes.

Writer and Activist. During the remaining years of the twentieth century, Walker continued to write best-selling novels and significant nonfiction works. Her collected poems appeared in 1991 as *Her Blue Body Everything We Know: Earthling Poems, 1965–1990*; *The Complete Stories* was published in 1994.

Walker also continued to fight for justice. She defended her own work against censorship, for instance, when some parents wanted to ban *The Color Purple* from use in the Oakland, California, public schools, and when others had two of her short stories removed from a California statewide examination. She crusaded against the abuse of women, whether it took the form of domestic violence or ritual mutilation, the subject of her book *Possessing the Secret of Joy* (1992) and of the documentary film and the book *Warrior Marks: Female Genital Mutilation and the Sexual Blinding of Women* (1993). Walker's lifelong habit of practicing what she preaches was illustrated by her asking that the bookstores she toured with her volume of activist essays, *Anything We Love Can Be Saved: A Writer's Activism* (1997), use her presence to raise money for local causes.

Walker and her husband, civil rights attorney Melvyn Leventhal, share a tender moment with their daughter, Rebecca Grant, in 1970. Walker's enormous respect and admiration for her mother is reflected in her daughter's middle name, Grant, which is Walker's mother's maiden name.

HIGHLIGHTS IN WALKER'S LIFE

1944   Alice Malsenior Walker is born on February 9 in Eatonton, Georgia.

1952   Loses sight in right eye after being shot accidentally.

1961   Enters Spelman College in Atlanta, Georgia.

1963   Transfers to Sarah Lawrence College in Bronxville, New York.

1964   Spends summer in Africa; has abortion after returning to Sarah Lawrence pregnant; has poems accepted for publication.

1965   Receives bachelor's degree from Sarah Lawrence; during summer, canvasses voters in Georgia; moves to New York City.

1966   Spends summer working for civil rights in Mississippi; meets Melvyn Rosenman Leventhal, returns with him to New York City.

1967   Marries Leventhal and moves with him to Jackson, Mississippi.

1968   Publishes *Once: Poems*.

1969   Daughter, Rebecca Grant, is born.

1970   Walker discovers the works of Zora Neale Hurston; publishes first novel, *The Third Life of Grange Copeland*.

1972   Moves temporarily to Massachusetts; teaches at Wellesley College and the University of Massachusetts-Boston.

1973   Father dies; Walker publishes three books.

1976   Divorces Leventhal.

1978   Moves to San Francisco; wins Guggenheim Fellowship.

1979   Publishes Zora Neale Hurston anthology.

1982   Publishes *The Color Purple*.

1983   Receives Pulitzer Prize and American Book Award for *The Color Purple*.

1985   Participates in filming of *The Color Purple*.

1992   Publishes novel *Possessing the Secret of Joy*.

1993   Writes, narrates, and coproduces film documentary *Warrior Marks*, an attack on female genital mutilation.

1997   Publishes *Anything We Love Can Be Saved: A Writer's Activism*.

WINNER OF THE PULITZER PRIZE
MORE THAN FIVE MILLION COPIES IN PRINT

ALICE WALKER

THE COLOR PURPLE

Alice Walker wrote works in a variety of genres, ranging from poems and short stories to essays and even a script for a documentary film. Although many of her shorter works are frequently anthologized, her novels, several of which were best-sellers, are more widely known.

Issues in Walker's Works. Walker's activism is reflected in her writings. She is best known as a black feminist, or as a *womanist,* the term she prefers. She crusades against the oppression of black women by the men of their own race, who use physical, sexual, and verbal abuse to keep women too fearful to oppose them or to find their own identities. Walker also worked to alert the world about the cruel and often lethal ritual of female circumcision, which is an accepted practice in many developing nations.

In her works Walker reminds her readers of the evils of slavery and of the racial injustice that persisted long after emancipation. She also took up the causes of other groups she believed to be treated unfairly, from racial equality in South Africa to the effects of the American embargo in Cuba. She is especially drawn to Native Americans because of their reverence for the environment, which became one of her primary concerns in the final decades of the twentieth century.

The Theme of Self-Realization. The second of the two epigraphs preceding *Anything We Love Can Be Saved* (1997) suggests that even death is preferable to slavery. However, it is clear that Walker is as much concerned about freedom for the spirit as she is about freedom from vio-

Walker expresses her support for a group of 175 individuals traveling to Cuba to challenge the U.S. ban on travel to that country at a press conference in San Francisco, California, on October 8, 1993.

Henry de Van Velde's painting *The Haymaker* (Musée du Petit-Palais, Geneva, Switzerland) depicts a modest woman carrying out hard work with simple means. Walker's mother's love for nature and ability to bring beauty to the family's ordinary surroundings helped secure a happy home for Walker, whose literary flower began to bloom under her mother's loving care.

lence and physical abuse. Many of Walker's women characters are never able to be themselves; they either live in fear of men or are merely under their control. Their frustration sometimes drives them away from their families. However, as Walker demonstrates in *Meridian*, mere distance is not enough to make a woman free. A woman must draw upon her inner strength, imitating those black women in the past who, even in slavery, would not allow their creativity to be stifled or their souls to be violated.

Walker's Importance. Alice Walker has been called the most important African American woman writer of the late twentieth century. This claim is based on her versatility and her large output, as well as on her popularity with both critics and the public.

However, since Walker's literary career showed no signs of slowing down at the century's end, it would be much too soon to make a final assessment of her significance. It does seem safe to assume that several of her short stories, her novel *The Color Purple*, and the film version of that work will continue to be taught in schools and colleges. It also seems clear that Walker herself will long be admired for her courage in raising issues that most people would rather ignore. In the 1990s, however, she seemed to be mellowing, replacing rage with a plea for love and understanding, moving from pessimism to optimism—indeed, to a new faith in humanity and a new vision of the future.

BIBLIOGRAPHY

Banks, Erma Davis, and Keith Byerman. *Alice Walker: An Annotated Bibliography, 1968–1986*. New York: Garland, 1989.

Bloom, Harold, ed. *Alice Walker: Modern Critical Views.* New York: Chelsea House, 1989.

Christian, Barbara T., ed. *Alice Walker: Everyday Use.* New Brunswick, N.J.: Rutgers University Press, 1994.

Gates, Henry Louis, Jr., and K. A. Appiah, eds. *Alice Walker: Critical Perspectives Past and Present.* New York: Amistad, 1993.

Gentry, Tony. *Alice Walker.* New York: Chelsea House, 1993.

Henke, Suzette A. "Women's Life-Writing and the Minority Voice: Maya Angelou, Maxine Hong Kingston, and Alice Walker." In *Traditions, Voices, and Dreams: The American Novel Since the 1960s.* Newark: University of Delaware Press, 1995.

Howard, Lillie P., ed. *Alice Walker and Zora Neale Hurston: The Common Bond.* Westport, Conn.: Greenwood Press, 1993.

Lauret, Maria. *Alice Walker.* New York: St. Martin's Press, 2000.

Tate, Linda. *A Southern Weave of Women: Fiction of the Contemporary South.* Athens: University of Georgia Press, 1994.

Washington, Mary Helen. "Alice Walker: Her Mother's Gifts." *Ms.* 10 (June, 1982): 38.

Winchell, Donna Haisty. *Alice Walker.* New York: Twayne Publishers, 1992.

SOME INSPIRATIONS BEHIND WALKER'S WORK

It is clear that Alice Walker considered her mother, Minnie, her primary inspiration. Minnie was always determined to do the best for her family. With flowers from her garden, she would transform the tenant shack where the family lived into a place of beauty. Similarly, after Walker's shooting accident, Minnie turned a tragedy into a positive experience, encouraging her daughter to spend her time reading and writing. No matter how tired she was, Minnie never called Walker from her reading to do household chores.

With her meager maid's earnings, Minnie bought her daughter three gifts, which Walker later realized had a symbolic significance as well as a practical purpose. The first, a sewing machine, enabled Walker to make her own clothes and thus become self-sufficient. The second, a suitcase, gave Walker her mother's "permission" to roam the world. The third, a typewriter, would always remind Walker that she had no excuse for not using her God-given writing talent. To Walker, her mother was both a role model and a representative of all black women everywhere who, with strength, wisdom, and love, have enabled the race to endure. Alice Walker has described her own work as a retelling of her mother's stories, so as to preserve a rich cultural heritage.

During her childhood, Walker responded to the poetic words from the Bible that she heard in church. In college, she became interested in the great Russian novelists, whom she admired for their skill in showing their characters against the backdrop of a specific society, as Walker does in her later novels. She was also drawn to writers with a feeling for fantasy and myth, such as the South American novelist Gabriel García Márquez, the Sioux Black Elk, and the African poet Okotp'tek. However, she found such African American writers as Jean Toomer, James Baldwin, Nella Larsen, Gwendolyn Brooks, and Zora Neale Hurston the most inspiring of all.

Walker posed for this photograph at her Berkeley, California, home in 2000. In her 2000 novel, *The Way Forward Is with a Broken Heart*, Walker confronts issues related to her ten-year-marriage and subsequent divorce from Melvyn Leventhal, a man who nurtured her talent and celebrated her heritage.

Filming The Color Purple: The Beginnings

On February 21, 1984, director Stephen Spielberg and composer Quincy Jones made a visit to Alice Walker's home in San Francisco, California, to discuss the filming of her novel *The Color Purple*. By the time the two men left, Walker felt certain that Spielberg understood her characters, and she knew that Jones would turn out a fine score for the movie. At first, Walker had intended to write the screenplay herself. However, after three months of working on it, she decided to turn the project over to someone else. In Menno Meyjes, Spielberg found someone who could manage the difficult task of turning an epistolary novel, written in the form of letters, into a dramatic script. Walker advised the production about sets, costumes, and local customs.

This movie still from *The Color Purple* captures a transformed Celie looking into the eyes of Shug, portrayed by actress Margaret Avery. Avery was relatively unknown in Hollywood before she landed the role of Shug.

This now classic silhouette from the film adaptation of *The Color Purple* epitomizes the loneliness and isolation of Celie, played by actress Whoopie Goldberg, before Shug comes along.

Walker was also involved in casting decisions and strongly believed that Whoopi Goldberg should play Celie. Walker had seen Goldberg perform, and Goldberg had written to her begging for the role. The author also urged Spielberg to consider some actors who were not big names in Hollywood, such as Margaret Avery, who was cast as Shug. However, Walker was probably proudest of using her influence on behalf of people who would never be stars. She insisted that half the production crew be black and female.

Novel into Film Script. Because Spielberg intended *The Color Purple* for a mass audience, he felt that it was important to make some alterations in Walker's story. For example, a lesbian love scene between Shug and Celie, which was quite explicit in the novel, was toned down so much that viewers might interpret it as a display of sisterly affection. Moreover, Mister, as played by Danny Glover, was much less threatening in the film than the cold-hearted man in the novel. In Shug's presence, Mister even became somewhat comical. Though Walker admitted that she could empathize with the film's version of Mister, she worried that this interpretation would make abusive men seem less dangerous and their deeds less horrifying. She also feared that Mister might replace Celie as the central figure in the story.

The most drastic change Spielberg made in Walker's work was in adding a subplot. Already he was pressed to condense into two and a half hours the narrative of events that took place on two continents over a period of three decades. Nevertheless, he felt that it was essential to modify the implications of Walker's so strongly pro-feminist (or pro-womanist), anti-patriarchal stance that was unsympathetic to traditional Christianity. In the film, Shug's father, the local minister, has nothing to do with his daughter because he disapproves of her lifestyle. Twice Shug is shown approaching him, begging for forgiveness, and twice he turns away from her.

All of this prepares for a huge production number late in the film, when Shug leads a parade of her friends and followers from the juke joint they frequent to the church where her father is conducting the Sunday service. The scene ends with a great reconciliation, father and daughter embracing, and saints and sinners joining in a spiritual. Thus, Spielberg's subplot contradicts not only the novelist's hostility toward Christianity but also her womanist antipathy toward patriarchy.

Reactions to the Film. Alice Walker commented that the first time she saw the film she hated it, and the second time, she loved it. The difference, she suggested, was that she was virtually alone at the initial viewing, while at the film's premiere there were hundreds of people sharing her experience. The fact that her retrospective book *The Same River Twice: Honoring the Difficult* is dedicated to Spielberg and Jones bears testament to Walker's often-stated belief that, all in all, the film did justice to the novel.

In most cases, the comments of reviewers say more about their own positions on controversial issues than about the film as an artistic creation. The conservative publication *Christianity Today* praised Spielberg for downplaying the lesbian implications of the book and for ending with Christian forgiveness and hope. In contrast, a reviewer for *The New Yorker*, a more liberal magazine, accused Spielberg of timidity and sentimentality. As the novel did, the film drew angry expressions from African American men. However, as Carol M. Dole points out, in the mid-1980s no one but Spielberg would have dared to make a film with an all-black cast and some uncomfortable truths, and nobody else could have made it so moving and delightful to mainstream audiences.

SOURCES FOR FURTHER STUDY

Digby, Joan. "From Walker to Spielberg: Transformations of The Color Purple." In *Novel Images: Literature in Performance,* edited by Peter Reynolds. London: Routledge, 1993.

Dole, Carol M. "The Return of the Father in Spielberg's The Color Purple." *Literature Film Quarterly* 24, no. 1 (1996): 12-16.

Dworkin, Susan. "The Strange and Wonderful Story of the Making of The Color Purple." *Ms.* 14 (December, 1985): 66-70, 94-95.

Walker, Alice. *The Same River Twice: Honoring the Difficult.* New York: Scribner's, 1996.

Whitaker, Charles. "Alice Walker: The Color Purple Author Confronts Her Critics and Talks About Her Provocative New Book." *Ebony* 47 (May, 1992): 86-88, 90.

Walker, who was relatively pleased with director Steven Spielberg's film adaptation of *The Color Purple*, is seen here at the after-movie party in the Hotel Pierre's Grand Ballroom in New York City on December 20, 1985.

THE COLOR PURPLE

Genre: Novel
Subgenre: Epistolary novel
Published: New York, 1982
Time period: The first half of the twentieth century
Setting: Rural Georgia; Africa

Themes and Issues. In *The Color Purple*, Alice Walker shows how African American women are abused both by whites and by the men of their own race. Walker stated that the story of her protagonist, Celie, was modeled on the experience of her own great-grandmother, who was raped and abused when she was twelve years old. Certainly two of the African American men in the story, Alphonso and Mister, or Albert, view women as objects to be used at will. This portrayal of African American men aroused much controversy when the novel first appeared. However, Walker does include two decent African American men in her book, Mister's son, Harpo, and Nettie's husband, Samuel. Even Mister improves in his latter years, or perhaps he just weakens with age.

The issue of racial injustice is taken up in a secondary plot. When Harpo's wife, Sofia, refuses to work for the mayor's wife, she is knocked down, thrown into jail, and then released into virtual slavery. This subplot is clearly meant to remind the reader that outside the homes in which African American men mistreat the women in their lives, there is a world where African Americans of both genders are often abused by whites.

The Plot. *The Color Purple* consists of seventy short letters, most of them written by Celie, a young black girl who lives in rural Georgia. While she is still too young to understand what is happening to her, Celie is raped repeatedly by her stepfather, Alphonso, whom she be-

Michael Graham-Stewart's watercolor *Slave with Her Mistress*, ca. 1820, captures the suppression of Celie, the heroine who is constantly forced to view herself through the eyes of someone else, in Walker's classic Pulitzer Prize–winning novel *The Color Purple*.

lieves is her real father. Inevitably, from time to time she becomes pregnant, but as soon as each baby is born, Alphonso disposes of it. Eventually Alphonso marries Celie off to Mister, who had asked for Celie's younger sister, Nettie. To get away from Alphonso, Nettie moves in with her sister. However, Mister turns out to be just as dangerous as Alphonso had been. When Nettie turns down Mister's advances, he kicks her out of the house. Cruelly, he even refuses to let Celie see the letters that Nettie sends her. Then Mister brings home his mistress, the singer Shug Avery, and asks Celie to nurse her back to health. At first Celie resents Shug, but before long the two women become friends and then lovers.

After Shug and Celie find letters from Nettie, describing her life in Africa, where she is mothering Celie's children as well as her own, Celie finds the strength to leave her husband and go with Shug to Memphis, Tennessee. There Celie develops her own business. Years later she returns to her family's home, which she inherited after Alphonso's death. She and a new, meek Mister become friends, and she is reunited with her sister and with her own lost children.

Analysis. Because most of the novel is written in dialect, *The Color Purple* may appear artless; in fact, it demonstrates considerable artistry. Critics have noted how much Celie's simple, ungrammatical language differs from the more

LONG FICTION

1970 The Third Life of Grange Copeland
1976 Meridian
1982 The Color Purple
1989 The Temple of My Familiar
1992 Possessing the Secret of Joy
1998 By the Light of My Father's Smile
2000 The Way Forward Is with a Broken Heart

SHORT FICTION

1973 In Love and Trouble: Stories of Black Women
1981 You Can't Keep a Good Woman Down: Short Stories
1994 The Complete Stories

POETRY

1968 Once: Poems
1973 Revolutionary Petunias and Other Poems
1979 Good Night, Willie Lee, I'll See You in the Morning: Poems
1984 Horses Make a Landscape Look More Beautiful
1991 Her Blue Body Everything We Know: Earthling Poems, 1965–1990

NONFICTION

1983 In Search of Our Mothers' Gardens: Womanist Prose
1988 Living by the Word: Selected Writings, 1973–1987
1993 Warrior Marks: Female Genital Mutilation and the Sexual Blinding of Women
1996 The Same River Twice: Honoring the Difficult
1996 Alice Walker Banned
1997 Anything We Love Can Be Saved: A Writer's Activism

SCREENPLAYS

1993 Warrior Marks

CHILDREN'S LITERATURE

1974 Langston Hughes: American Poet
1988 To Hell with Dying
1991 Finding the Green Stone

EDITED TEXT

1979 I Love Myself When I Am Laughing . . . and Then Again When I Am Looking Mean and Impressive: A Zora Neale Hurston Reader

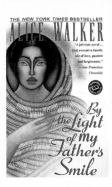

abstract and correct speech of her highly educated sister. Moreover, Celie's own language changes as the novel proceeds. At the beginning of the story, her speech reflects a child's innocence and a child's certainty that God, to whom she is writing, will find a way to rescue her. After Shug enters her life, Celie begins to change. At first she seems shocked by Shug's irreverence and especially by her outspokenness about sex. Soon, however, Celie can also joke about men, women, and even her own body. As Celie's sense of humor develops, so do her capacity for analysis and her sense of self, which enable her at last to gain her own independence.

SOURCES FOR FURTHER STUDY

Fifer, Elizabeth. "The Dialect and Letters of *The Color Purple*." In *Contemporary American Women Writers: Narrative Strategies*, edited by Catherine Rainwater and William J. Scheick. Lexington: University Press of Kentucky, 1985.

Gates, Henry Louis, Jr., and K. A. Appiah, eds. *Alice Walker: Critical Perspectives Past and Present*. New York: Amistad, 1993.

Johnson, Yvonne. *The Voices of African American Women: The Use of Narrative and Authorial Voice in the Works of Harriet Jacobs, Zora Neale Hurston, and Alice Walker*. New York: Peter Lang, 1998.

Ross, Daniel W. "The Making of Celie in Alice Walker's *The Color Purple*. In *Teaching American Ethnic Literatures: Nineteen Essays*. Albuquerque: University of New Mexico Press, 1996.

HER BLUE BODY EVERYTHING WE KNOW: EARTHLING POEMS, 1965–1990

Genre: Poetry
Subgenre: Confessional free verse
Published: San Diego, 1991
Time period: Late twentieth century
Setting: United States; Africa

Themes and Issues. As the title indicates, *Her Blue Body Everything We Know: Earthling Poems, 1965–1990* includes poems that Walker wrote over a twenty-five-year period. In the preface to this collection, Walker notes that as she prepared it for publication, she had to decide whether or not to make any changes. She was inclined to alter some of the earlier poems. After all, she was no longer the same person as the troubled young girl who honestly expected to kill herself or the young woman consumed by passion for her lover. In the end, however, Walker wisely decided to let her poems stand as they were written. What remained constant over the years, Walker points out, was the healing power of poetry. It was poetry that assured her of her own value, that time after time gave her a reason to live on.

The Poems. *Her Blue Body Everything We Know* is made up of Walker's four previously published collections, along with a final section entitled "We Have a Beautiful Mother: Previously Uncollected Poems." Each of the earlier collections is preceded by a new introduction, in which Walker reflects on her experiences at the time she was writing those particular poems. *Once: Poems* was a product of Walker's college years, though it was not published until after she had graduated. Her second collection, *Revolutionary Petunias and Other Poems* (1973), arose out of her experiences in Mississippi. *Goodnight, Willie Lee, I'll See You in the Morning: Poems* (1979) and *Horses Make a Landscape Look More Beautiful* (1984) both appeared after Walker moved to California.

Analysis. While the poems in this collection are impressive in themselves, they can be read also as a record of Walker's intellectual and emotional development. *Once: Poems* is a volume filled with the passion of youth. In the African poems, there is a fierce joy in nature. Other poems in the volume reflect Walker's sense of betrayal by men and by her own body. *Revolutionary Petunias* reflects Walker's commitment to the civil rights struggle but also her awareness that the very revolutionaries she admires are often contemptuous of ordinary southern blacks and, moreover, that many black males are guilty of sexism.

For the title of *Good Night, Willie Lee, I'll See You in the Morning: Poems*, Walker used the last

Oh, which way to go? The horse in Franz Marc's 1910 *Horse in the Landscape* (Essen Museum, Germany) contemplates the wide, open space that lies ahead of her, or possibly him (but more likely her), before determining which direction to take. The warm yellows and greens seem to paint a bright future, though, as Walker's collection *Horses Make a Landscape Look More Beautiful* ultimately does.

words her mother spoke to her father. In this volume, Walker often looks back to Georgia and to her childhood, and she tries to understand why the relationships between men and women are so often destructive. In *Horses Make a Landscape Look More Beautiful*, Walker expresses her concern about the environment, which she sees as desperately imperiled by human greed and self-indulgence, but she also voices her hope that the power of love and a new appreciation of nature will save the world she finds so beautiful.

SOURCES FOR FURTHER STUDY

Russell, Sandi. *Render Me My Song: African-American Women Writers from Slavery to the Present*. New York: St. Martin's Press, 1990.

Sanoff, Alvin P. "The Craft of Survival: *The Color Purple* Book Author Alice Walker on Writing Verse." *U.S. News and World Report* 110 (June 3, 1991): 51.

Winchell, Donna Haisty. *Alice Walker*. New York: Twayne Publishers, 1992.

IN LOVE AND TROUBLE: STORIES OF BLACK WOMEN

Genre: Short fiction
Subgenre: Social realism
Published: New York, 1973
Time period: Twentieth century
Setting: Southern United States; New York City; Uganda, Africa

Themes and Issues. The thirteen stories in Walker's first published collection all deal with injustice and/or betrayal. In most of the stories, black women are the victims. Sometimes the villains are black men, who assume that women are placed on this earth for their use. At other times, they are white men or women, who, having been reared in a racist society, obviously consider African Americans unworthy of respect or compassion. Some of the stories have an element of folklore or magic. Throughout the book, Christianity is pre-

Alice Kent Stoddard's representation on a young black man in *Young Man in Blue Suit*, ca. 1930, is a stark contrast to Walker's meditations on black men. Stoddard reveals little about the thoughts of her subject, while Walker analyzes, dissects, and exposes the black man in his society, often reaching less than flattering conclusions about his motives and his actions toward black women.

sented as a faith that defrauds and deceives black people.

The Stories. Most of the short stories in *In Love and Trouble* end unhappily. In "The Child Who Favored Daughter," a young girl is mutilated by her father so that she will not become involved with a lover. In "Roselily" and "'Really, *Doesn't* Crime Pay?,'" women are destroyed by men who regard them as objects existing solely for their use.

Some of the stories show how a single incident of cruelty or neglect can destroy an individual or a family. In "Strong Horse Tea," a white postman neglects to send a doctor to a sick child, as he had promised to do, and the child dies. In "The Revenge of Hannah Kemhuff," a white welfare worker refuses aid to a hungry family, eventually causing the deaths of not only the children but also the heartless worker herself.

Although there is a certain poetic justice in the ending of that story, only one work in this collection has a truly happy ending. The narrator of "Everyday Use" is a mother torn between her desire to please her successful, selfish daughter, Dee, and her sweet-tempered daughter, Maggie. Dee, who has taken an African name, has come home to claim two of the family quilts, which she had once scorned but now considers fashionable. Dee says that Maggie does not deserve the quilts because she does not appreciate her cultural heritage. At that point, the narrator knows what she must do; she snatches the quilts out of Dee's arms and gives them to Maggie, who clearly loves her mother and her family far more than Dee ever will.

Analysis. As the subtitle indicates, *In Love and Trouble: Stories of Black Women* is not primarily about racial injustice but about the mistreatment of black women in our society. By the time these stories were published, a great many voices had been raised to protest the treatment of African Americans. Some activists noted the involvement of certain so-called Christians in the most un-Christian actions; Walker herself was outspoken in her insistence that Christianity itself was a false faith.

What shocked black men about Walker's stories was her portrayal of them as abusers of women. Although Walker could admit that black men might be venting the frustrations resulting from their own oppression in a racist society, Walker would not excuse men who mistreated women.

It is probably significant that the stories in this collection that are most often found in anthologies do not deal with either the failures of Christianity or the defects of black men. "Everyday Use" is about a conflict between three African American women, and "To Hell with Dying" is a touching story about a beloved elderly black man.

SOURCES FOR FURTHER STUDY

Hubbard, Dolan. "Society and Self in Alice Walker's *In Love and Trouble*." In *American Women Short Story Writers: A Collection of Critical Essays*. New York: Garland, 1995.

Petry, Alice Hall. "Alice Walker: The Achievement of the Short Fiction." *Modern Language Studies* 19 (Winter, 1989): 12–27.

Wade-Gayles, Gloria. "Black, Southern, Womanist: The Genius of Alice Walker." In *Southern Women Writers: The New Generation*, edited by Tonette Bond Inge. Tuscaloosa: University of Alabama Press, 1990.

Other Works

LIVING BY THE WORD: SELECTED WRITINGS, 1973–1987 (1988). Alice Walker's second volume of essays includes seventeen selections written from 1973 to 1987. For her epigraph, she chose a passage from an African author, Ayi Kwei Armah, which ends with one of Walker's primary themes: the need for wholeness. The selections in *Living by the Word* deal with both the wholeness of the individual and the wholeness of the community, but as the au-

Massimo Campigli's 1928 painting *The Amazons* reflects Walker's fascination with the relationship between horses and human beings, which she expresses from the horse's perspective in her essay "Am I Blue?," part of her 1988 collection of essays, *Living by the Word*.

thor explains in her preface, these two kinds of wholeness are interrelated. This book is highly personal, chronicling a journey from place to place and also through time and memory, undertaken so that the author could become closer to the earth and the creatures upon it.

Walker's subjects vary. There are observations of nature, such as "Am I Blue?," in which she comes to understand a horse's feelings about human beings, as well as thoughts about animal rights and vegetarianism. Sometimes Walker focuses on events that leave her outraged, such as a deadly 1985 fire in Philadelphia, Pennsylvania. At times she writes about her own family, as she does in "Father"

and also in an essay about her daughter's smoking. Sometimes she describes people she admires, such as her Native American friend Bill Wahpepah. Sometimes she chronicles her travels, whether to China, Jamaica, or her old home in Georgia. Often she makes useful comments about her own works.

The essays vary as much in form as in subject matter. Some of them were originally speeches, while others are her own meditations. There is even an occasional poem. From time to time, there is a section listed as a journal entry. The end of the book, while serving as a vehicle for the author's deepening self-knowledge, allows the reader to know her as well.

MERIDIAN (1976). As the story of a young woman's coming of age during the turbulent 1960s, *Meridian* draws upon Alice Walker's own experiences and to some degree is an autobiographical work. Like Walker, the title character, Meridian Hill, attends college in Atlanta, Georgia, and then in the North. She, too, later returns to the Deep South to work in the Civil Rights movement. However, Meridian Hill had been married young and had a child and does not have the support from her mother that Walker had from hers. Meridian's mother makes her children feel guilty for having been born. It is hardly surprising that Meridian does not know how to love her own child.

In Atlanta, Meridian becomes involved with a young revolutionary, who makes her question her dedication to the cause and then cavalierly discards her for a white girl, whom he marries. Although Meridian continues her work in the rural South, she is sick in body and soul. She feels that she has been a failure as a daughter and as a lover, and because she was never certain that she could kill for her cause, she also feels like a failure as a revolutionary. At the end of the novel, however, Meridian emerges a well woman, with a new commitment to life and a new sense of self that enables her to forgive her ex-lover.

POSSESSING THE SECRET OF JOY (1992). The central character in *Possessing the Secret of Joy* is Tashi, who appeared in *The Color Purple* as the Olinka girl who was the best friend of Celie's daughter Olivia. However, Walker insists that the later novel is not meant as a sequel to the earlier one. In *The Color Purple*, Tashi was a minor character; in *Possessing the Secret of Joy*, she is the major figure.

The book is complex and sometimes confusing. Walker begins by having Tashi speak from beyond the grave, then turns the narrative over to other characters, each of whom has a somewhat different interpretation of what happened to her. It is obvious that Tashi's tragedy began with a wrong choice. Even though her own sister Dura bled to death after a ritual female circumcision, Tashi decides to have the procedure performed on her in honor of her cultural heritage. Tashi changes her name to Evelyn Johnson when she moves to the United States with her minister-husband, but she cannot change the fact that her operation has made sexual relations difficult and childbirth almost impossible. After her son is born developmentally disabled, Tashi falls into depression and then madness.

The outline of the African woman in Elizabeth Barakah Hodges's 1995 painting *Africa* seems to slip away into the backdrop of the painting, echoing Tashi's tragic loss of wholeness and control in Walker's compelling novel *Possessing the Secret of Joy*.

Finally, Tashi returns to Africa and kills M'Lissa, the woman who was responsible for so many female circumcisions and for Dura's death. Because the Olinkan male leaders revere M'Lissa as a woman who helps them to maintain their power over women, they sentence Tashi to death. Tashi, however, has found the inner peace she was seeking by taking action against evil. Walker has said that she hopes this book and her other efforts will help to end female genital circumcisions on the African continent.

Resources

Sources of interest to students of Alice Walker include the following:

Voice of the Shuttle. The English department at the University of California, Santa Barbara, maintains a meta-Web site called "Voice of the Shuttle," with bibliographies of English and American literature. Under the "Minority Literatures/Afro-American" headings are several Web sites devoted to Alice Walker. (http://vos.ucsb.edu/shittle/eng-min.html#afro-american)

Voices from the Gaps: Women Writers of Color. An Internet research project devoted to the works of American women writers of color features a page on Alice Walker, with a biography, a selected bibliography, criticisms, and related links. (http://voices.cla.umn.edu/authors/AliceWalker.html)

Audio Recordings. Several audio recordings are available in which Alice Walker reads her work or discusses issues important to her. The American Audio Prose Library offers both *Alice Walker Reading 'Nineteen Fifty-Five' and Interview* (1981) and *An Interview with Alice Walker* (1981) by Kay Bonetti.

Sounds True in Boulder, Colorado, has recorded both *My Life as Myself: An Intimate Conversation* (1995), read by Alice Walker, as well as *Giving Birth, Finding Form* (1993), in which three women writers—Walker, Isabel Allende, and Jean Shinoda Bolen—talk about women and creativity.

Video Recordings. Schlessinger Video Productions offers a program on *Alice Walker* (1994), produced and directed by Rhonda Fabian and Jerry Baber, in its *Black Americans of Achievement* series. In *Black and White: Conversations with African American Writers: Part 4* (1992), by the California Newsreel company of San Francisco, there is "A Conversation with Alice Walker." Sounds True produced the video *Pama Chodron and Alice Walker in Conversation: On the Meaning of Suffering and the Mystery of Joy* (1999), in which Walker and Pama Chodron, a American who is now a Tibetan Buddhist nun, discuss an ancient meditation technique they have both found valuable.

ROSEMARY M. CANFIELD REISMAN

Index

Page numbers in **boldface** type indicate article titles. Page numbers in *italic* type indicate illustrations.

Accidental Tourist, The (Tyler), 1541, 1545,
　　1546, 1548, 1550, 1551, 1552, *1553*
Africa (painting), *1581*
After Tea (painting), *1472*
Amazing Grace (Terkel; play), 1521
Amazons, The (painting), *1580*
America (painting), *1524*
American Dreams: Lost and Found
　　(Terkel), 1522, 1523, 1524–25,
　　1528, 1532, *1533*, 1534
"Am I Blue?" (Walker), 1580
"Anecdote of the Jar" (Stevens), 1480, 1481
Anything We Love Can Be Saved: A
　　Writer's Activism (Walker), 1565,
　　1566, 1567, 1575
Auroras of Autumn, The (Stevens),
　　1470, 1471, 1475, 1485–86
Automobile Industry (mural), *1537*

Ballo della Vita, Il (painting), *1483*
Baptism (painting), *1503*
"Benjamin Reid: Aftermath" (Styron), 1504
Benton, Thomas Hart, *1502*
Bierstadt, Albert, *1533*
Breathing Lessons (Tyler), 1541, 1545,
　　1546, 1551, 1554–55
Bunker, John S., *1559*
Bustling City (painting), *1479*

Caffè Florian (painting), *1556*
Campigli, Massimo, *1580*
Cannery, 1931, The (painting), *1465*
Cannery Row (Steinbeck), 1448, 1450,
　　1452, 1454, 1465
"Carnet de Voyage" (Stevens), 1469, 1471
Cathedral Forest (painting), *1533*
Celestial Navigation (Tyler), 1544,
　　1549, 1551, 1557–58
Chicago (Terkel), 1522, 1523
Chinese Siamese Cat, The (Tan), 1508,
　　1509, 1514, 1517
Clark, Joseph, *1554*
Clock Winder, The (Tyler), 1544, 1548,
　　1550, 1551
Collected Poems of Wallace Stevens, The,
　　1470, 1471, 1475, 1486, 1487
Colorful Landscape with Aquatic Birds
　　(painting), *1484*
Color Purple, The (Walker), 1561, 1564–65,
　　1566, 1568, 1570–76, 1581
Coming of Age: The Story of Our
　　Century by Those Who've Lived It
　　(Terkel), 1522, 1523, 1537–38

Confessions of Nat Turner, The (Styron),
　　1489, 1492, 1494, 1496,
　　1497–1500, 1504
Crowd XX (painting), *1548*
Cup of Gold (Steinbeck), 1447, 1451, 1454

Dali, Salvador, *1486*
"Darkness Visible" (Styron), 1496, 1500
Darkness Visible: A Memoir of Madness
　　(Styron), 1489, 1493
"Death-in-Life of Benjamin Reid, The"
　　(Styron), 1504
Destiny 1 (painting), *1550*
Dinner at the Homesick Restaurant (Tyler),
　　1541, 1545, 1546, 1551, 1555–57
Division Street: America (Terkel), 1521,
　　1522, 1523, 1524, 1531, 1538, 1539

Earthly Possessions (Tyler), 1548,
　　1549, 1551, 1558
East of Eden (Steinbeck), 1448, 1452,
　　1454, 1466
Eckel, Julia, *1497*
Edwards, Mary Ellen, *1538*
"Emperor of Ice-Cream, The"
　　(Stevens), 1480, 1481
"Endgame" (Tan), 1507–8
"Esthétique du Mal" (Stevens), 1487
Esthétique du Mal (Stevens), 1471, 1475
"Everyday Use" (Walker), 1579

Factory at Horta de Ebro (painting), *1474*
"Farewell to Florida" (Stevens),
　　1482–83
"Father" (Walker), 1580
films, 1445, 1447, 1448, 1449, 1453,
　　1455–56, *1457*, 1458, *1459*,
　　1460, 1462, 1464, 1466, 1493,
　　1506, 1508, 1509, *1513*, 1541,
　　1545, 1561, 1564, 1565, 1566,
　　1568, 1570, *1571*, 1572–73
Flower of the Flock, The (painting), *1554*

Giants of Jazz (Terkel), 1521, 1522,
　　1523, 1524, 1539
"Gift, The" (Steinbeck), 1464–65
Good Night, Willie Lee, I'll See You in
　　the Morning: Poems (Walker),
　　1575, 1576–77
"*Good War, The*": *An Oral History of*
　　World War II (Terkel), 1522, 1523,
　　1524–25, 1528, 1532, 1538, 1539
Graham-Stewart, Michael, *1574*

Grapes of Wrath, The (Steinbeck),
　　1445, 1448, 1450, 1451, 1452,
　　1453, 1454, 1455–56, *1457*,
　　1458, 1462–64
Great Divide, The: Second Thoughts on
　　the American Dream (Terkel),
　　1522, 1523, 1526, 1532, 1534
Green Leaf and the Sere, The (painting),
　　1538
Gropper, William, *1537*

Hard Times: An Oral History of the
　　Great Depression in America
　　(Terkel), 1522, 1523, 1524–25,
　　1528, 1532, 1534–36, 1538
Harmonium (Stevens), 1467, 1470,
　　1471, 1473, 1475, 1480–82,
　　1486
Haymaker, The (painting), *1568*
Her Blue Body Everything We Know:
　　Earthling Poems, 1965–1990
　　(Walker), 1565, 1575, 1576–77
Hodges, Elizabeth Barakah, *1581*
Horse in the Landscape (painting), *1577*
Horses Make a Landscape Look More
　　Beautiful (Walker), 1575, 1576, 1577
Hundred Sweet Senses, The (Tan), 1508,
　　1509, 1511, *1512*, 1514, 1517
Hurston, Zora Neale, 1564, 1566,
　　1569, 1575

"Idea of Order at Key West, The"
　　(Stevens), 1482, 1483
Ideas of Order (Stevens), 1470, 1471,
　　1473–74, 1475, 1482–83
If Morning Ever Comes (Tyler), 1543,
　　1546, 1551
I Love Myself When I Am Laughing...and
　　Then Again When I Am Looking
　　Mean and Impressive: A Zora Neale
　　Hurston Reader (Walker ed.),
　　1564, 1566, 1575
In Love and Trouble: Stories of Black
　　Women (Walker), 1564, 1575, 1577–79

Johnson, William H., *1499*
Joy Luck Club, The (Tan), 1505, 1507,
　　1508, 1509, 1511, 1512,
　　1513–15, 1517, 1518
Joy Luck Club, The (Tan; screenplay),
　　1506, 1508, 1509, *1513*

Kennington, Dale, *1556*

Kitchen God's Wife, The (Tan), 1508, 1509, 1511–12, 1514, 1515–16

Ladder of Years (Tyler), 1545, 1548, 1551
Lange, Dorothea, *1463*
Langston Hughes: American Poet (Walker), 1564, 1575
Lee, Anna Belle, *1503*
Lemmers, Georges, *1472*
Letters of Wallace Stevens (H. Stevens ed.), 1471, 1475
Lie Down in Darkness (Styron), 1491, 1492, 1494, 1495, 1500, 1502–3
Living by the Word: Selected Writings, 1973–1987 (Walker), 1575, 1579–80
Long March, The (Styron), 1491, 1495, 1500

Man with the Blue Guitar and Other Poems, The (Stevens), 1470, 1471, 1474, 1475
Marc, Franz, *1577*
Martin, Donald, *1553*
Meridian (Walker), 1564, 1568, 1575, 1581
Metzinger, Jean, *1484*
Missouri family on Highway 99 (photograph), *1463*
Mocialskij, D. K., *1547*
Modarressi, Mitra, 1545, 1546
"Moon Lady, The" (Tan), 1517–18
Moon Lady, The (Tan), 1508, 1509, 1514, 1517–18
Morgan's Passing (Tyler), 1545, 1548, 1551
Morse, Samuel French, 1475
Mountain Lake (painting), *1486*
Munch, Edvard, *1483*
My American Century (Terkel), 1522, 1538

Nat Turner (painting), *1499*
Necessary Angel, The: Essays on Reality and the Imagination (Stevens), 1471, 1475, 1486–87
"Notes Toward a Supreme Fiction" (Stevens), 1487–88

O'Brien, Smith, *1465*
Of Mice and Men (Steinbeck), 1450, 1452, 1453, 1454, 1456, 1460–62
Okamoto, Naoki, *1512*
Once: Poems (Walker), 1563, 1566, 1575, 1576
Ong, Diana, *1524*, *1548*, *1550*
Opus Posthumous (Stevens; Morse ed.), 1471, 1475, 1487

Parts of a World (Stevens), 1470, 1471, 1475
Patchwork Planet, A (Tyler), 1545, 1546, 1551, 1558–59

Pearl, The (Steinbeck; novel), 1448, 1454, 1462, 1465–66
Pearl, The (Steinbeck; screenplay), 1453, 1454
"Personal Memoir (and parenthetical comment), A" (Terkel), 1534
Picasso, Pablo, *1474*
Portrait (In Middle Age) (collage), *1553*
Possessing the Secret of Joy (Walker), 1565, 1566, 1575, 1581–82

Qian, Zifen, *1511*
Quattro Generazioni (painting), *1547*

Race: How Blacks and Whites Think and Feel About the American Obsession (Terkel), 1522, 1523, 1526, 1534, 1539
"Really, *Doesn't* Crime Pay?" (Walker), 1579
"Red Candle, The" (Tan), 1514
Red Pony, The (Steinbeck), 1447, 1452, 1453, 1454, 1462, 1464–65
Red Pony, The (Steinbeck; screenplay), 1453, 1454
"Revenge of Hannah Kemhuff, The" (Walker), 1579
Revival (painting), *1497*
Revolutionary Petunias and Other Poems (Walker), 1564, 1575, 1576
Ricketts, Edward F., 1447, 1448, 1451, 1452, 1454, 1465
"Rock, The" (Stevens), 1474, 1486
"Roselily" (Walker), 1579
"Rules of the Game" (Tan), 1507

"Sad Strains of a Gay Waltz" (Stevens), 1482, *1483*
Saint Maybe (Tyler), 1545, 1551
Same River Twice, The: Honoring the Difficult (Walker), 1572, 1575
Schuenke, Susanna, *1485*
Sea of Cortez (Steinbeck and Ricketts), 1447, 1454
Sea of Time, The (painting), *1485*
Searching for Caleb (Tyler), 1544, 1551, 1559–60
Self-Portrait with Rita (painting), *1502*
Set This House on Fire (Styron), 1491–92, 1494, 1495, 1496, 1500
Shahn, Ben, *1526*
Sickles, Peter, *1479*
Sky Simulated by Red Flamingoes (painting), *1473*
Slave with Her Mistress (watercolor), *1574*
Slipping-Down Life, A (Tyler), 1544, 1551
Sophie's Choice (Styron), 1489, 1493, 1494–95, 1496, 1500–1502
Spectator, The: Talk About Movies and Plays with Those Who Make Them

(Terkel), 1522, 1523, 1527–28, 1530
Springtime Angel (painting), *1559*
Steinbeck, John, **1445–66**
Stevens, Holly Bright (daughter), 1470, 1471, 1475, 1478, 1482
Stevens, Wallace, **1467–88**
Stoddard, Alice Kent, *1578*
"Strong Horse Tea" (Walker), 1579
Styron, William, **1489–1504**
"Sunday Morning" (Stevens), *1472*, 1473, 1480, 1481, 1482
Sunny Day with Gentle Breeze, A (painting), *1511*

Talking to Myself: A Memoir of My Times (Terkel), 1522, 1523, 1528
Tan, Amy, **1505–18**
Terkel, Studs, **1519–40**
Thayer, Abbott Handerson, *1473*
Their Blood Is Strong (Steinbeck), 1448, 1454, 1455–56
Third Life of Grange Copeland, The (Walker), 1564, 1566, 1575
This Quiet Dust (Styron), 1500, 1503–4
Tibaldi, Pellegrino, *1515*
Tidewater Morning, A: Three Tales from Youth (Styron), 1493, 1500
Tin Can Tree, The (Tyler), 1543, 1546, 1551
Tortilla Flat (Steinbeck), 1447, 1450, 1453, 1454, 1459–60, 1462
Transport to Summer (Stevens), 1470, 1471, 1475, 1487
Travels with Charley: In Search of America (Steinbeck), 1448, 1454
Tumble Tower (Tyler), 1545, 1546, 1551
Tyler, Anne, **1541–60**

Ulysses and His Companions on the Island of Cyclops (painting), *1515*
Unemployment (painting), *1526*

Van Velde, Henry de, *1568*

Walker, Alice, **1561–82**
Warrior Marks (Walker; screenplay), 1566, 1575
Warrior Marks: Female Genital Mutilation and the Sexual Blinding of Women (Walker), 1565, 1575
Way Forward Is with a Broken Heart, The (Walker), 1569, 1575
Working: People Talk About What They Do All Day and How They Feel About What They Do (Terkel), 1522, 1523, 1524–25, 1527, 1536–37

Young Man in Blue Suit (painting), *1578*